BACK AT THE DOJO

Lally Katz

Currency Press, Sydney

BELVOIR

CURRENT THEATRE SERIES

First published in 2016
by Currency Press Pty Ltd,
PO Box 2287, Strawberry Hills, NSW, 2012, Australia
enquiries@currency.com.au
www.currency.com.au

in association with Belvoir, Sydney

Cataloguing-in-publication data for this title is available from the National
Library of Australia website: www.nla.gov.au

Typeset by Dean Nottle for Currency Press.
Cover design by Alphabet Studio.
Cover image shows Natsuko Mineghishi, Dan Katz and Luke Mullins. (Photo by
Brett Boardman)

Contents

Theatre Program at the end of the playtext

Currency Press acknowledges the Traditional Owners of the Country on which we live and work. We pay our respects to all Aboriginal and Torres Strait Islander Elders, past and present.

Back at the Dojo was first produced by Belvoir and Stuck Pigs Squealing at Belvoir St Theatre, Sydney, on 22 June 2016, with the following cast:

JERRY / others	Fayssal Bazzi
BROWN BELT / others	Dara Clear
LOIS / others	Catherine Davies
DANNY (younger)	Harry Greenwood
DAN (older)	Brian Lipson
SENSEI	Natsuko Mineghishi
PATTI	Luke Mullins
PAMELA / CONNIE / others	Shari Sebbens

Director, Chris Kohn
Set and Costume Designer, Mel Page
Lighting Designer, Richard Vabre
Composer and Sound Designer, Jethro Woodward
Dramaturgs, Louise Gough and Anthea Williams
Karate Consultant, Natsuko Mineghishi
Consultant, Transgender Victoria
Producer Stuck Pigs Squealing, Nina Bonacci
Voice Coach, Suzanne Heywood
Stage Manager, Mel Dyer
Assistant Stage Managers, Keiren Smith and Lyndie Li Wan Po
Directorial Secondment, Olivia Satchell

Commissioned by Stuck Pigs Squealing, with funding support from the Australia Council for the Arts and Creative Victoria.

Australian Government

Australia Council for the Arts

CREATIVE VICTORIA

CHARACTERS

DAN KATZ, elderly

DANNY, Dan as a younger man

MARTY, Danny's brother

SAMMY, Danny's brother

LOIS, a young woman

CONNIE, Lois's sister

PATTI, Dan's grandchild

MARTIN, Danny's father

ALICE, Danny's mother

JERRY, Lois's brother

SENSEI, a karate teacher

NURSE

BARTENDER

MAN IN BAR

LECTURER

GUY IN LECTURE

SOUTHERNER

HIPPY GUY

JUDGE

BROWN BELT, a karate enthusiast

STUDENTS, HIPPIES, KARATE STUDENTS, POLICEMAN, MENTAL HOSPITAL GUARD, MENTAL HOSPITAL PATIENTS, PARTYGOERS

SETTING

The play is set in New Jersey and the Southern States of America in the late 1960s and in present-day Australia.

This play went to press before the end of rehearsals and may differ from the play as performed.

ACT ONE

SCENE ONE

DAN KATZ, *an older man, is in a room in an Australian hospital. An elderly woman,* LOIS, *lies in the hospital bed. She is not conscious.* DAN *is doing* karate katas. *Over and over again. He looks like he may have been doing them for hours. There is no way of telling how long he has been in there. In between each kata he stops and looks over at the bed. He sees nothing has changed.* LOIS *is still not conscious. He begins the next kata.*

A NURSE *comes in. She clears her throat.* DAN *doesn't hear her. She steps into the room.*

NURSE: Mr Katz?

DAN: Oh! Hi, sorry, Pamela.

NURSE: Mr Katz, are you sure you don't want us to have a bed made up in here for you?

DAN: Oh, no thanks, Pamela. Very nice of you, but those cots kill my back.

NURSE: You have to get some sleep. I don't think you've left her bedside the whole time your wife's been here.

DAN: Don't worry about me.

NURSE: Well, I'm going on dinner break, but if you change your mind, just ring the bell and Sarah will be only too happy to bring you one in.

DAN: Thanks, Pamela. I really appreciate it.

NURSE: Don't exhaust yourself in here.

DAN: Oh no, it's good, I get too cramped up just sitting.

NURSE: We, you've got a lot of energy. We're all marvelling about it. We thought you were angry at first because of the way you're always punching the air.

DAN: Oh, no—it's just habit.

NURSE: We can see that now. It's kung fu you're doing?

DAN: No, I've never known kung fu. Never in my life. Only *karate*.

NURSE: Oh—well, that's even better! Japanese. I hope they're all okay now.

DAN: Pardon?

NURSE: After that awful tsunami. I haven't heard much. It's funny, the news. Headlines don't seem to last anymore.

DAN: No. I guess not. There's always something new.

NURSE: Well, see you later.

> *The* NURSE *is leaving. She turns around.*

I'll bet she sure appreciates you being here, Mr Katz.

DAN: I want to be here when she wakes up.

> *He looks at her.*

When will that be?

NURSE: Mr Katz, I'm sorry. You know I can't answer that.

> DAN *nods.*

DAN: I know, Pamela.

> *The* NURSE *leaves.*

> DAN *stands. Begins to punch the air. Kicks the air. Not aggressively. Just like practice. But all the while, his focus is on* LOIS *in the bed. He does* karate *kata after* karate kata, *often making vocal noises that go with them, not even realising he's doing it.*

> PATTI *enters the hospital room. Perhaps she stops just in the doorway. She seems surprised to see* DAN, *kicking and punching the air. Perhaps, for a moment, she thinks about leaving.*

PATTI: Grandfather. Dear Grandfather. It is I, the prodigal grandchild, returned home.

> DAN *looks up.*

DAN: Hello, Patrick.

PATTI: It's Patti now. P-A-T-T-I.

DAN: You should have said you were coming.

PATTI: I sent you a text.

DAN: We don't know how to use texts.

PATTI: Grandma sent me one once. But it just said the letter 'H'.

DAN: She must have done it by mistake.

PATTI: Well, I don't have any diseases in case that's what you're wondering. Not even a cold—so I'm perfectly safe around a hospital.

Pause.

I didn't leave because I'm an asshole. I just thought it would make it easier. It's very hard, you know, being around the people who keep seeing you in the wrong way.

DAN: You just do whatever is good for you, Patti.

PATTI: Thank you. I will. Do you think Grandma can hear us?

DAN: Of course.

PATTI: Good. I want her to know I'm here. That I care. That I'm not a completely repugnant person.

DAN: You can talk to her if you want.

PATTI: Hi, Grandma.

Silence.

It's me. Patti. Sorry I've taken so long to come in.

She looks at him.

Do you think she knows it's taken me this long to visit?

DAN: Grandma doesn't keep score.

PATTI: Everyone keeps score.

DAN: Not Grandma.

PATTI: Can I sit down with you and Grandma for a while?

DAN: Do whatever you want, Patti.

> PATTI *sits.* DAN *gets up and does some stretches. He punches the air.* PATTI *doesn't watch him. She keeps her eyes down.*

Are you on drugs, Patti?

PATTI: What?

DAN: Are you tripping?

PATTI: What—no.

DAN: Your pupils are huge. Look at me.

> PATTI *looks down.* DAN *stands over* PATTI.

Look at me.

PATTI: No.

DAN: Look at me.

> PATTI *takes a moment, then looks up at him.*

PATTI: It's just because I've gone from being outside to inside. Anyone who does that, their pupils are huge.

DAN: You are. You're tripping.

PATTI: Talk about being dramatic. I am not tripping. God.

DAN: How can you do that? How can you do that to us? Come in here—
on drugs?

PATTI: Grandpa—I am not— Why is it always about what I do to other
people—why is it that my actions are always making everyone
miserable? And then I go—and that's wrong too. And then I come
back and that's worse. I'm just trying to be a human. God.

DAN: You should go, Patti.

PATTI: You don't know the night I've had. You don't know the night I've
had and you're turning me out. Fine. Fine.

DAN: Are you having a bad trip, Patti?

PATTI: No, Grandad.

DAN: Tell me what happened.

PATTI: Nothing. Nothing happened.

DAN: What are you seeing?

PATTI: I'm not seeing anything. Why do you think I'm seeing anything?
I'm not tripping.

DAN: I can tell.

PATTI: Okay. Okay. I'm gonna go.

> *She gets up.*

DAN: Don't go, Patrick.

PATTI: Did you call me that on purpose?

DAN: What?

PATTI: Patrick.

DAN: No. It's habit. It's your name.

PATTI: It's not my name anymore. It's Patti now. It's not that hard. With
a double-T, I. Like Patti Smith. Just like Patti Smith.

DAN: Who's Patti Smith?

PATTI: You're kidding me?

DAN: What?

PATTI: How can you not know who Patti Smith is?

DAN: I just don't.

PATTI: She's from New Jersey.

DAN: Really?

PATTI: Like you. Like Grandma.

DAN: I didn't know her.

PATTI: You sure?

DAN: Yeah.

PATTI: She's my hero.

DAN: What does she do?

PATTI: She's only one of the most influential artists of your time.

DAN: Like a painter?

PATTI: Yeah—she does artwork, but she's a singer, Grandpa.

DAN: Okay. Would I like her?

PATTI: I think so.

DAN: What does she sing?

PATTI: I'd sing you something, but I'm tone deaf.

DAN: I know.

PATTI: Isn't it ironic—the one thing I want to do in this world is sing. And I'm born tone-deaf.

She hums to herself for a moment.

Man, I wish I could sing her songs.

She hums again, dances a little.

DAN: What are you on?

PATTI: Nothing. You asked me what she sings. I can't do anything right. Everything I do is messed up.

DAN: You're having a bad trip.

PATTI: I'm not. My life is a bad trip. First I was born in the wrong body. Well, the body's not bad—except for one little detail. Listen, I know what you're thinking. But I didn't come here to make this about me. I came to see Grandma. And you … I wish it could still be like when I was little. You guys were always so happy to see me when I was little.

DAN: Of course we were happy to see our grandson.

PATTI: But now I'm not the me that you loved, is that right? I'm not your grandson.

DAN: I still love you, Patti.

PATTI: Then why are you angry at me?

DAN: Because your behaviour is terrible.

PATTI: So was yours, when you were my age. I know it was. Okay, maybe younger than me. True, I'm no spring chicken anymore. God, time goes fast.

DAN: That doesn't bother me.

PATTI: Getting older doesn't bother you?

DAN: I never used to like the past.

PATTI: But that's where you met Grandma.

DAN: Yeah.

PATTI: And she's still there. She's here too—but mostly, she's back there now.

> DAN *doesn't answer. He begins a kata.* PATTI *puts her hand on* LOIS*'s hand in the bed. She watches* DAN *for a moment, then looks down again.*

SCENE TWO

Time has changed. It's the late sixties. DANNY KATZ, *as a young man, is in a New Jersey bar. He sits at the bar, his two brothers,* MARTY *and* SAMMY, *are with him.*

DANNY: I got fake ID and they won't card you guys 'cause you're so tall. Look, it's my real name and everything—Daniel Katz.

SAMMY: But, Danny, I'm fifteen.

DANNY: Keep it down, Sammy.

> *He walks up to the bar. He says to the woman tending the bar:*

I'll take three bourbons and cherry coca colas please.

BARTENDER: Anything else, hon?

DANNY: Nope. Thanks.

BARTENDER: Coming right up.

> *She pours three tall bourbons and puts in a splash of coke, some cherry juice, and a cherry in each glass. Hands them to the three brothers. She goes back to her bar tending.*

> DANNY *and his two brothers gather together, drinking their bourbons.* SAMMY *and* DANNY *begin to drink.* MARTY *looks at his.*

DANNY: See. Drink up, Marty.

> MARTY *picks up the glass and swallows some down.* DANNY *finishes his. He goes to the bar.*

Another round please.

The BARTENDER *pours them.* MARTY *and* SAMMY*'s drinks are lined up behind their current ones.* DANNY *begins to gulp back his second one.*

MARTY: You pitched a good game, Danny.

DANNY: Nah. My arm's gone dead.

SAMMY: What does that mean?

DANNY: It means I'll never pitch another good ball.

MARTY: I don't think that's true.

DANNY: You heard what Father said.

MARTY: He doesn't know baseball. Only tennis.

SAMMY: He thinks baseball is just like tennis. But it's different.

DANNY: Well, either way, we got killed.

MARTY: I still say you pitched a good game.

SAMMY: Do they have pretzels here?

DANNY: Don't ask for pretzels.

SAMMY: I'm hungry.

DANNY: They'll card you if you ask for pretzels.

SAMMY: They gave me bourbon without carding me.

DANNY: Pretzels are pushing it.

MARTY: Danny …

DANNY: Yeah?

MARTY: Do you think we should head home soon?

DANNY: Go if you want.

MARTY: It's just that Mother and Father—

DANNY: I don't care.

SAMMY: We don't want to miss dinner.

DANNY: Go home. If you don't like the bar, go home.

MARTY: I'll stay.

DANNY: No. Go. I want to be alone.

MARTY: I'll stay.

DANNY: I said go.

MARTY: We'll tell Mother and Father you're with the team.

DANNY: They'll know I'm not. Not after that game.

MARTY: You pitched a good game, Danny.

DANNY: Fuck baseball.

SAMMY: We'll try and save you a plate in the fridge.

MARTY *and* SAMMY *leave.*

DANNY *finishes his drink and then drinks theirs. He goes to order another. A* MAN *stands up from a bar stool on the other side of the bar. He is older. His arm is in a sling. His hair is longish—scraggly. He looks messed up. He calls out to* DANNY.

MAN: I got a dead arm too, son.

He raises his glass to his arm in a sling.

DANNY: What happened to you?

The MAN *calls out to the* BARTENDER.

MAN: I'll have what my young friend is having. And so will he.

The BARTENDER *pours them both a glass. The* MAN *raises his glass to* DANNY *across the bar.* DANNY *raises his back.*

Salute.

DANNY *copies him.*

DANNY: *Salute.*

The MAN *drinks.*

MAN: Coca cola. Cherry coca cola. That's nice. I forgot how nice a sweet taste can be.

He comes and sits by DANNY.

This town is a friggin' stranger, you know, son. You read me, son? This town makes me too lonesome to do the great stand. 'Cause I was gonna. You read me, son? I get it. I get the whole situation. I get the whole damned world. And I was gonna take it on. All of it. I was gonna call the revolution.

DANNY: I don't understand.

MAN: You do, I think. I think you might be the only one in this damn bar that does understand.

DANNY: I'm the only one in the bar.

MAN: It's 'cause you and me, we both got a dead arm. They killed my arm. And they filled me up with lonely—up to here.

He motions to his throat—to his Adam's apple.

Right up to my Adam's apple. That's how they stop you. Those of us who can see the truth. That's how they stop us from spreading the truth. They isolate us. They'll try and do it to you.

DANNY: Listen—

MAN: Don't say you're gonna go. Have one more drink with me. I gotta warn you. 'Cause I know you. I know your eyes. They'll be comin' to get you.

DANNY: Who?

MAN: The government. They'll track you down, son, now that your arm is dead. They're gonna have their spies and their employees offer you LSD.

DANNY: What's that?

MAN: That's what they done to me. I coulda—what I saw—I coulda started the revolution. But now I can't—because I'm so goddamned lonely. You promise me. You promise, boy—when they offer it to you—you say no thanks. And you get the hell out of town. You won't know them at first. They'll seem like your friends. Or maybe they'll be men of science. Could be they're posing as farmers. But when they offer it to you, you leave town. Got it?

DANNY: Okay.

MAN: You promise—when they come to you and they try to connect your mind—you say no. Because it'll be the last connection you ever have, son. You promise me.

DANNY: Yeah. Yeah, sure. I promise.

MAN: Don't you ever let them make you take LSD.

> *A young woman,* LOIS, *comes into the bar with her sister,* CONNIE. DANNY *looks up from the* MAN. *He is captivated by* LOIS. *He stands up.* CONNIE *says to the* BARTENDER:

CONNIE: Two manhattans please.

BARTENDER: Do you have ID?

CONNIE: Of course.

> *She looks through her purse.*

Hmmm. I must have left it in the car. Lois, do you have yours?

> LOIS *is looking down–she can't help but giggle. She and* DANNY *catch eyes.*

LOIS: I think mine is in the car too.

CONNIE: We'll just go out and get our IDs.

> *They rush out, laughing uncontrollably. They are gone.* DANNY *watches after them.*

SCENE THREE

PATTI *is sitting wide awake, eyes wide open, looking down at* LOIS. DAN *is up, stretching.* PATTI *jumps.*

DAN: What? What?
PATTI: Nothing. It was nothing, Grandad.
DAN: Did she move? Did you see her move?
PATTI: No. I just thought …
DAN: Are you sure?
PATTI: No.
DAN: Get the nurse.
PATTI: I was probably just seeing stuff.
DAN: Get the nurse.

> PATTI *runs out.* DAN *sits by* LOIS.

Lois? Loiey? Can you hear me? Loiey? It's Dan. It's Danny, Lois. Can you hear me?

> PATTI *comes back in with the* NURSE. *The* NURSE *is calm. She walks in,* PATTI *behind her.* PATTI *is breathing heavily.*

NURSE: What happened, Mr Katz?
DAN: My uh—Patti—thought he—she thought Lois moved her mouth.
PATTI: I wasn't sure. I was probably seeing things.
NURSE: Let me check.

> *The* NURSE *holds* LOIS*'s eyes open, shines a small flashlight in. Checks her pulse. Looks at the machine reading. She looks up.*

Not this time, Mr Katz.
DAN: Right.
NURSE: But it's good to have a moment of high spirits I think. It lifts the whole room.

> *The* NURSE *leaves.* PATTI *and* DAN *stand, staring at each other.*

PATTI: I'm sorry.
DAN: You're tripping. Aren't you?

SCENE FOUR

New Jersey. A college classroom. The LECTURER/TUTOR *is speaking to the class.*

LECTURER: So any thoughts about *Moby Dick*?

> *Nobody says anything.* DANNY *walks into class. His eyes are red. He's very stoned.*

Danny, where are you up to in the book?

DANNY: Uh, which book?

LECTURER: Which book? The book. The big book.

DANNY: The Bible?

LECTURER: Ha ha. No, Danny. Not the Bible. *Moby Dick.*

DANNY: Oh, yeah. I like the whale.

> *The* LECTURER *looks closer at* DANNY.

LECTURER: Danny, are you sick or something? Your eyes are all red.

DANNY: Yeah. I got a cold.

> *The rest of the class sniggers.*

LECTURER: Well, don't sit near me, I'm going camping this weekend. Last thing I want is a cold out there fishing on the river.

> DANNY *goes and sits next to another* GUY.

GUY: I wouldn't mind some of your cold. You got any left? For after?

> DANNY *laughs.*

I'm serious. I can't study now unless I'm high.

DANNY: You waste being high on studying?

GUY: Well, somebody's gotta read *Moby Dick*.

DANNY: The whale wins.

> DANNY *and the* GUY *laugh.*

I'm tired of studying all the time—trying to be somebody else's idea of smart. I think I like seeing things better my own way.

GUY: Who doesn't? But your own way doesn't pay the bills.

DANNY: Everything always comes down to paying the bills. You know what? I don't give a damn—I won't pay them.

> *The* GUY *laughs. The* LECTURER *turns to them.*

LECTURER: Something funny you want to share with the rest of us about *Moby Dick*?

DANNY: Just funny how obsessed he is with a whale. When the whale probably never thinks about him at all. That's life. A lot of our energy gets given to something big. Something so big that it doesn't know we exist. But it still takes our energy. The machine of life just drinks us like oil.

LECTURER: Interesting point, Danny. When you actually come to class you're an interesting participant.

SCENE FIVE

New Jersey. DANNY KATZ *is maybe a year or so older than before. Maybe about nineteen years old. He sits across from* MARTIN, *his father.*

MARTIN: So you're a college dropout.

DANNY: I haven't dropped out. I'm taking a year off.

MARTIN: You're a dropout.

DANNY: I've been in school my whole life. I want to get some actual experiences.

   ALICE, *his mother, comes into the room.*

ALICE: The Strongs' eldest is in his third year of medical school. He's going to have very interesting life experiences.

MARTIN: You know what kind of experiences you're going to have dropping out of college, Danny? The same ones over and over again. Working in menial jobs with other college dropouts.

DANNY: I haven't dropped out.

MARTIN: Stop with the BS. At least call it what it is.

ALICE: If you go back you're going to be older than the other students. You'll be out of step.

MARTIN: You should enlist in the army.

DANNY: I'm not going to Vietnam.

ALICE: Your father fought in World War Two.

MARTIN: And it made me the man I am.

DANNY: I'm not you. I'm not enlisting.

MARTIN: What a waste.

SCENE SIX

New Jersey. DANNY KATZ *is packing his bag.* MARTY *watches him.*

MARTY: Where you gonna go?
DANNY: Don't know.
MARTY: How will you get there?
DANNY: I'll hitch.
MARTY: Do you need any money? I've got some money. From Aunt Rose
    for my last six birthdays. I've got seventy-five dollars.
DANNY: You keep it.
MARTY: I don't need it for anything.
DANNY: Keep it.
MARTY: When will you come back?
DANNY: In a while.
MARTY: Will you stay with Freddy in New Orleans? Is that where you're
    going?
DANNY: For a while I most probably will.
MARTY: That's good. Freddy's at college, right?
DANNY: Right.
MARTY: That's good. Does he know you're coming?
DANNY: Sure.
MARTY: And you know where he lives, right? And you've got a number
    for him?
DANNY: Sure.

    He picks up his bag.

Okay. 'Bye 'bye.

    DANNY *goes to leave.* SAMMY *comes in.*

SAMMY: Dinner's ready. You having dinner before you leave, Danny?
DANNY: Nah. I gotta hit the road.
SAMMY: You want a container to take with you?
DANNY: Sure.
SAMMY: I'll tell Mother.

    SAMMY *leaves.*

MARTY: What are you lookin' for, Danny?
DANNY: Shut up.

MARTY: I don't mean that bad—not in a bad way—

    DANNY *leaves.*

SCENE SEVEN

Karate dojo. *A Japanese* karate SENSEI *takes his shoes off. Bows. Enters the* karate dojo. *With a cloth, he begins to clean the floor. After cleaning the floor, he mediates on his knees.*

SCENE EIGHT

DANNY *travels through the roads of America. He is walking along with his thumb out. Smoking a joint. A car stops by him. A guy, with a cowboy hat, leans out.*

SOUTHERNER: What you doin' in the south, boy?

DANNY: Passin' through.

SOUTHERNER: How long you been passin' through for?

DANNY: A while.

SOUTHERNER: You ain't hitchhikin', is you?

DANNY: I was.

SOUTHERNER: 'Gainst the law round here, son.

DANNY: My mistake.

SOUTHERNER: You ain't one of them hippies, is you?

DANNY: No, sir.

SOUTHERNER: I hate them hippies. Yankee hippies.

DANNY: I'm not a hippy.

SOUTHERNER: You need a haircut, boy. Growin' long around the ears.

DANNY: Thanks for pointing it out.

SOUTHERNER: Funny tobaccy you's smokin' there, boy.

DANNY: Is it?

SOUTHERNER: I always carry a gun with me, son. Watch out, son. 'Cause round here, if the negroes don't getcha, the KKK will.

DANNY: And which one might you be?

SOUTHERNER: I'm just a hospitable southerner. Whatever you're lookin' for, Yankee, you ain't gonna find it here. Good evening to ya, son.

DANNY: You too, sir.

    The SOUTHERNER *drives away.*

SCENE NINE

DANNY *is walking through the farmlands of Kentucky. He's with a friend—who's a real hippy-looking* GUY. DANNY's *hair has gotten quite long.*

GUY: Wild hemp plants. Farmers don't even know they're sitting on a goldmine. They just take their rifles and shoot at us 'long hairs'. They don't even know they're sitting right on the revolution. They got no insight, man.

DANNY: They're stuck in the old way. Old world. They ain't seein' nothing. They don't even open their eyes to what the possibility could be, man.

    The GUY *stops.*

GUY: Do you feel that?

DANNY: What?

GUY: I felt it. I felt the world turning. You feel that?

    DANNY *stops. Thinks. Feels.*

DANNY: I do.

GUY: All the time the world is turning, but most people don't ever feel it, their whole life.

DANNY: That is the saddest thing. Think about that. Living your whole life here—and always feeling still—always feeling like it's stuck— nothing's stuck, man—nothing is stuck. They just tell us that it has to be. But we can be anything. We can be fluid. We can just be motion, man.

GUY: Right on, Danny. Right on.

DANNY: We're on the crest of this. We're on the crest of the new brain of the world. We are thinking with the turning of the world. Our brains are turning in our heads like the world is turning in outer space.

    DANNY *stops and turns very slowly in a circle. The* GUY *laughs. He stops and turns very slowly in a circle too.*

GUY: But you know what—you know what? Right here in America— our minds are turning—but not the land of the free, man. The land of the free is stuck like fuck. Do you feel that? Do you feel all our brains turning in America, but America just stuck?

DANNY: It's like dried mud. Like a clump of dried mud. Or a lump of concrete in the bottom of a swamp.

GUY: But it used to be something different, man. It used to be alive. This country used to be alive. When it was the Indians', it was alive. And they said it was going to be free. Our forefathers said it was going to be free. But it was a trap. The worst trap of all. The *Mayflower* should have sunk. America is a prison. But people like you and me, Danny, our minds are still turning.

DANNY: Yeah. We're turning.

GUY: Hey, you feel that?

DANNY: I feel something—I feel something—someone watching—

GUY: On your right. Old farmer has a gun aimed at us.

DANNY: Of course he does. Let him shoot. He won't though. Fuck America.

GUY: Keep walking, Danny.

SCENE TEN

PATTI *is sitting over* LOIS. DAN *is* karate *punching and kicking the air.*

DAN: So where exactly have you been, Patti?

PATTI: Tonight?

DAN: No, for the past two years.

PATTI: I've been living with someone. I've been to love and back. What a swell place it was. I guess you have a lot of questions—such as—who was this mystery man? Was he good enough for my grandchild? Was he a kind man? Where is he now? The truth is, Grandad—he wasn't very interesting at all. You know, he'd never been with a man before. He wasn't gay. He loved me for being a woman. I thought I'd like that. I thought that was what I was looking for. Finally, I could be the person I was inside. But you know, Grandad—I found it a depressing role, all in all. Being a girlfriend. I was always waiting for him. Did you know men are like that? They like to have women waiting for them. He'd never answer his phone when I called it. He'd call me back in about half an hour and his voice would be distant. Like he was talking to me from behind a wall. And when he'd come home, he'd just sit on the net for hours. Presumably looking up porn. It was very interesting to arrive where I thought I'd been heading and find it wasn't for me. I don't think being a woman is like that for Patti Smith. But of course, I was madly in love with him. And miss him desperately every waking minute of the day and night. I suppose my constant anxiety didn't exactly draw us closer. Towards the end—I felt like I was Maggie the Cat—you know—from *Cat On A Hot Tin Roof*—I was always hanging around trying to seduce him—to pique his interest. Life is so disappointing.

DAN: When did you break up?

PATTI: The day before yesterday. It turns out he doesn't think he can love me. It seems his ex-girlfriend Lydia is coming back into the picture. Lydia is not exactly fat, but she is also very not thin. To be honest, Grandad—I feel so awful about the whole thing. I feel so awful about everything.

    The NURSE *comes in. She checks* LOIS.

DAN: Can I ask you a favour, Pamela?

NURSE: Sure.

DAN: Are there any oranges that we could have?

NURSE: Yes, we have oranges. Not for Mrs Katz—

DAN: Oh, no—they're for Patti.

NURSE: I'll see what I've got.

    The NURSE *leaves.*

PATTI: What do I want oranges for?

SCENE ELEVEN

DANNY *is sitting in a rundown house with some other hippies. They are smoking pot.* DANNY *is taking tabs of acid.*

The world starts to turn on him. He looks at the faces of the people he is with. One at a time, they come out from the world. He doesn't like, doesn't trust them.

One of the guys' mouth moves, but words from somewhere else come out:

GUY: We are nothing. You are nothing. You hate America? But you are America. You're everything ugly about America. Selfish hippy. You want everything for yourself. You're not a real citizen of anywhere.

    DANNY*'s words are garbled too.*

DANNY: That's not true, man.

GUY: You're a piece of shit. And every minute that you're living you're breathing shit into the air. You're breathing shit in and you're breathing shit out. Your mouth is a farting anus. Sucking farts in. Burping farts out. You are America.

DANNY: I am. I am. I am America.

> *The* GUY *starts talking normally. He did not hear or realise he was participating in the other conversation. It was just* DANNY *who was seeing it and hearing it.*

GUY: Hey, Danny, why so serious?

> DANNY *shrugs.*

DANNY: Just thinking.

GUY: You look like you're at college. You're not at college though, Danny. You're in the college of life. You dropped out of the rat-race and you got enlightened, man.

DANNY: I didn't drop out of anything.

GUY: Don't hold onto bullshit, man. Man, I've got a fucking leg cramp.

> *He stretches out his leg. Can't quite do it.*

Fuck, Danny, can you stretch my leg out?

> DANNY *looks at him. A* GIRL *there comes and stretches his leg out.*

Can you suck me off while you're there?

GIRL: For a joint.

GUY: Okay. But we've only got leaf left.

> *He begins to undo his fly. He laughs.*

Fuck America—right, Danny?

DANNY: Right.

> *The* GIRL *breathes in from the joint and says:*

GIRL: I want some lemonade—who's gonna get me some lemonade? Danny?

> DANNY *looks away from her.*

DANNY: No—I don't have any lemonade.

> DANNY *stands up. Goes to walk outside.*

OTHER GUY: Where you goin', Danny?

DANNY: For a walk.

OTHER GUY: What for?

DANNY: I just … I wanna find some oranges.

GIRL: Oranges—don't eat oranges, Danny—they'll take away your high.

DANNY: I gotta go get some oranges.

GUY: What you lookin' for, Danny?

GIRL: He's lookin' for something out there.

OTHER GUY: Nothin' out there, Danny, but southerners. Stay in here, man.

GUY: Stay in here, Danny, and we'll see the world.

DANNY: No. I see it, man. I already see it.

GUY: Tell us. Tell us what you see.

DANNY: We're all pieces of shit.

GUY: Don't turn on the revolution, Danny.

DANNY: You're nothing. I'm nothing.

GUY: Don't you bring us down, Danny. You fucker. Don't you bring us down.

> DANNY *runs out onto the street.*
>
> *Out on the street, he looks around, madly. A Southern man walks by him. Wearing a cowboy hat.*

DANNY: Excuse me—sir—you know where I can get some oranges—or just one orange?

> *The man turns around. It's the same man from the car before—or at least to* DANNY *it is.*

SOUTHERNER: Yeah, come with me, Yankee. I got some oranges.

DANNY: Oh, sorry—I gotta go—I got some oranges back someplace else—

SOUTHERNER: Go to the general store, Yankee. Anything else you looking for out here, hippy?

SCENE TWELVE

In the dojo. *A young man,* JERRY *is there, alone. He is training by himself. He looks like he's been there for a long time. Practising his kata—Heian Shodan—over and over again. He has a slightly club foot, turned in a little—he is trying to work his way around it in the kata. He is getting frustrated by it.*

The SENSEI *enters. He watches* JERRY*'s kata.*

CONNIE, *his sister, comes in. She's a young woman now in high-waisted jeans.*

CONNIE: Jerry, me and Lois are waiting in the car. Hurry your little butt up.

JERRY: Just ten more minutes, Con.

CONNIE: Okay.

> CONNIE *exits.* JERRY *goes back to the kata.*

JERRY: *Heian Shodan!*

> *He does the kata. He does it well, but his club foot gets in the way. He stops.*

It's useless. I can't.

SENSEI: Have I said you can't?

JERRY: No.

SENSEI: Who are you to decide you can't?

JERRY: *Oss*, Sensei.

SENSEI: *Heian Shodan!*

JERRY: *Heian Shodan!*

> JERRY *begins the kata again.* LOIS *stands in the doorway. She watches him.*

> SENSEI *nods to her. She smiles.*

> JERRY *finishes the kata. He bows to* SENSEI.

SENSEI: Better. Never say you can't. You don't know. But your body knows. Clean up and then go, your sister is waiting.

LOIS: It's no rush! We don't have to be anywhere.

SENSEI: No, we are finished. Never keep the lady waiting.

> LOIS *smiles, shyly.*

> JERRY *bows to the* SENSEI *and begins to clean the floor.* JERRY *finishes and comes up to* LOIS.

JERRY: Hey, Lois.

LOIS: Looking good, bro.

JERRY: No, I'm not. I suck.

LOIS: You do not! You're really coordinated.

JERRY: Coordination's for girls.

LOIS: Hey!

> *She laughs and punches him. He laughs too.*

You're practising so much. I'm impressed.

JERRY: No matter how much I practise it's not going to change my foot.

LOIS: Well, I think you're really good.

JERRY: Yeah, but you just think that because I'm your favourite.

LOIS: You are my favourite actually. Don't tell Connie.

JERRY: Sorry, but I'll have to tell Connie. She should know. Man, she's gonna be pretty mad.

LOIS: You're probably her favourite too.

JERRY: Yeah, but that's *her* favourite. That doesn't mean she wants me to be your favourite. Look, as long as you two don't make me pick.

LOIS: Never! But seriously, Jerry, I'm impressed. You're really good.

JERRY: Thanks, sis.

LOIS: You feel like pizza?

JERRY: Always.

> *They leave the* dojo.

SCENE THIRTEEN

YOUNG DANNY KATZ *is sitting in a jailhouse. He's sitting behind bars. Quietly losing his mind. Sweating. Totally quiet. A* POLICEMAN *comes and opens the door. The* POLICEMAN *has a deep, southern accent.*

POLICEMAN: Judge'll see ya now.

> DANNY *stands up. The* POLICEMAN *comes in, handcuffs him, and walks him to the courtroom, which is just down the hall. The* JUDGE *is sitting at the bench.*

Here he is, Judge Arnold.

> *The* JUDGE *looks up.*

JUDGE: This is the fellow that you caught breaking the window at the general store?

POLICEMAN: Yes, sir.

JUDGE: Okay, Sam, we'll be okay from here.

POLICEMAN: Could be he's still dangerous.

JUDGE: We'll be okay. Thanks, Sam.

POLICEMAN: Well, I'm gonna be just outside the door now.

Sam, the POLICEMAN, *walks outside the door.*

JUDGE: Approach the bench please, son.

DANNY walks up to the bench.

What you doin' in Kentucky now?

DANNY: I was working on a ranch.

JUDGE: Now I know you ain't a cowboy.

DANNY: No, I don't ride. Just a ranch hand, that's all.

JUDGE: How long you been working at this ranch for, son?

DANNY: One month.

JUDGE: You still working there?

DANNY: No, sir.

JUDGE: Why not?

DANNY: Just moved on, that's all.

JUDGE: Maybe you moved on too soon if you need to break into the general store. But what you didn't figure on is that Fox Mathers doesn't keep one cent of cash on his premises when he closes up for the night.

DANNY: With all due respect, Your Honour, I wasn't after trying to get cash.

JUDGE: What were you breaking in for?

DANNY: For groceries, Your Honour.

JUDGE: Groceries? Bread? Milk?

DANNY: Just for oranges.

JUDGE: Oranges?

DANNY: Yes.

JUDGE: What on earth were you doing breaking in there at two a.m. looking for oranges for?

DANNY: I had a hankering.

JUDGE: Are you mentally ill?

DANNY: No.

JUDGE: Don't lie to me now. You're under oath.

DANNY: Am I?

JUDGE: I didn't swear you in?

DANNY: No, Your Honour.

JUDGE: You know why that is?

DANNY: Why?

JUDGE: It wouldn't do no good. What does a Jew care about swearing in on the Bible?

DANNY: I don't take any issue with the Bible.

JUDGE: Neither do I. I swear folks in on it every day. Okay now, that's an exaggeration—not enough crimes committed or folks suing folks here for me to swear someone in even once a month—but when it happens, I do it. I don't take offence to the Bible either.

DANNY: You're Jewish?

JUDGE: Only Jewish judge in the state.

DANNY: I'm not religious.

JUDGE: Doesn't matter. I don't care if you're religious or you ain't. What I'm asking you, son, is are you mentally ill?

DANNY: No, I'm not.

He stops and thinks.

JUDGE: Don't lie to me.

DANNY: I'm not mentally ill. But I'm not well. Not too well right now either.

JUDGE: You're going to tell me why you were breaking into the general store. Tell me the truth. You're under my oath, son. You're talking to the only Jewish judge in the state.

DANNY: I was looking for oranges.

JUDGE: But why?

DANNY: Because they have Thorazine in them.

JUDGE: What did you want Thorazine for?

DANNY: They say it's an antidote to LSD.

JUDGE: LSD?

DANNY: Hallucinogens. I was taking hallucinogens.

JUDGE: What for?

DANNY: To seek out the truth. To find something, I suppose.

JUDGE: Jews don't take drugs. And we don't get tattoos. It goes against our fundamentals. Do you understand what I mean by that, son?

DANNY: Yes. I think I do.

JUDGE: You had a real bad time, didn't you, son?

DANNY: Yes, Your Honour. I had a real bad time.

JUDGE: How long you been taking these hallucinogens for?

DANNY: Over one year, Your Honour.

JUDGE: And last night, that's when it turned inside out on itself? Is that right?

DANNY: Yes, Your Honour.

JUDGE: What did you see, son?

DANNY: I saw my friends, Your Honour. I saw the selfishness in them. Then hopelessness. But worse—worse—

JUDGE: What did you see in yourself, son?

DANNY: I'm nothing. I'm nothing. I saw that I'm nothing. Not even a blade of grass. Everything I thought till now—everything I said— did—it was nothing—I left my body. I was outside my body looking in at it—and it was nothing. And the Earth—the Earth, Your Honour, is a big, cold place. No sympathy from the Earth—only disdain. I felt the disdain of the Earth—of the sky—for my body. For my mind—I was outside in the Earth—looking in at me—I was the Earth's disdain, Your Honour. And I was as lonely as I've ever been.

JUDGE: What happened, son, is you were taken by God. But you never had any Jewish training, did you?

DANNY: No, Your Honour.

JUDGE: God took you back. Adon was always there. You were always a Jew. He tapped you on the shoulder, cold and angry. And he took you back. Now I'll ask you again, young Jewish man, what are you doing in Kentucky?

DANNY: I was working.

JUDGE: What are you doing, young, Jewish man, in Kentucky? It's not the place for you.

DANNY: I see.

JUDGE: Where are you from?

DANNY: New Jersey.

JUDGE: Ah, yes. That's better.

DANNY: I don't know if it is.

JUDGE: Oh, it is. You've got to go back there now. And get some discipline. God is with you now, whether you are in synagogue or not. But if you aren't going to follow his rules and laws exactly, then you got to get yourself another form of discipline. You understand me, son?

DANNY: Yes, Your Honour.

JUDGE: You play a sport?

DANNY: I played baseball till my arm went dead.

JUDGE: You look like an athlete.

DANNY: I got no skill.

JUDGE: Well, that's up to you to decide. So long as you decide on somethin'. Now I'm gonna let you go—no fine. Nothing, young Jewish man. But you have to catch the Greyhound bus back to New Jersey. I can't never see you in Kentucky again.

DANNY: Yes, Your Honour.

JUDGE: You got the bus fare?

DANNY: No, Your Honour.

JUDGE: Well, then. Guess I'll have to take you to the station and get you a ticket myself. 'Least that way I know you're on the bus.

SCENE FOURTEEN

On the Greyhound bus. DANNY *sits alone. Staring out the window. He passes the nightmares of America.*

But perhaps also the beauty of America. It passes PATTI, *standing with a small suitcase on the side of the road. And the* SENSEI, *doing* karate, *singing.* JERRY *tries to copy, but can't get the moves. He gets frustrated, but the* SENSEI *motions not to worry.* DANNY *sees them, but doesn't understand.*

The bus stops. A very fat MAN *comes and sits next to* DANNY. *They are squashed together. The fat* MAN *holds out a bag of corn chips.* DANNY *looks at the corn chips hopefully. The fat* MAN *begins to eat them. He eats the whole bag.*

They pass the nightmares of America through the window of the Greyhound bus.

SCENE FIFTEEN

DANNY KATZ *walks up the driveway to his house.* MARTIN *is outside, shearing a bush.*

DANNY: Hello, Father.

MARTIN: Danny, what a surprise.

DANNY: I just got back.

MARTIN: Will you be moving back into your bedroom?

DANNY: No, I just came by to let you know I'm back here.

MARTIN: Where will you live?

DANNY: In Trenton.

MARTIN: Trenton?

DANNY: Yeah, I got a little apartment there.

MARTIN: How do you expect to pay the rent?

DANNY: I'll work, like everybody else.

MARTIN: I thought you were too big to be like everybody else.

DANNY: I never said that.

MARTIN: You know the Strong boys are all in college now. Jed's graduated.

DANNY: Congratulations to him.

MARTIN: Well, you may as well come in for dinner. What's happened to your eyes?

DANNY: Nothing.

MARTIN: They look darker than they used to.

DANNY: Well, I can't see my own eyes.

SCENE SIXTEEN

In the hospital room, PATTI *is sitting, eating an orange, piece by piece.* DAN *is watching* LOIS.

PATTI: What are you gonna do, Grandad?

> DAN *looks at* PATTI.

What are you gonna do when Grandma dies?

DAN: She'll wake up soon.

PATTI: Did the doctor say that?

DAN: The nurse seems to think it.

PATTI: The nurse seems like one of those people that wants everybody to feel okay.

DAN: Don't talk like that in here. She can hear you, remember?

PATTI: I don't think she'd mind. I think she'd want me to ask these questions. She wouldn't want you to keep waiting for her to wake up, if she's not going to.

DAN: I spent the beginning of my life waiting for her. Before I'd met her. Then after I met her. And I don't want to stop waiting now.

PATTI: My boyfriend's name was Rex. That's like a dog's name. Why would someone name their son a dog's name? What kind of set-up are they giving him for life? It's funny. Longing. I longed for someone so much. Then I met him and I longed for him when I was with him. Because he wasn't really there. And now that I'm away from him, I long for him back again. I guess that's the biggest trick of life. To either stop longing. Or stop minding it.

She eats another piece of orange.

I like this orange.

She sighs.

You have no idea, Grandpa, what it's like to live in constant disapproval from the people you love.

SCENE SEVENTEEN

DANNY, SAMMY *and* MARTY *all sit at the dinner table. Also at the table are their parents,* MARTIN *and* ALICE. *They have been eating in silence.* SAMMY *is helping himself to seconds.*

MARTIN: And did you meet any of Freddy's friends at college, Danny?
DANNY: Sure. I met a few of them.
ALICE: Were they nice?
DANNY: Sure. They were okay.
ALICE: Did they know that you dropped out of college?
DANNY: I dunno. Maybe.
ALICE: Were they too polite to ask?
DANNY: They probably just didn't care one way or the other.
MARTIN: Did they ask you what you were doing with your life?
DANNY: It wasn't a job interview, Father. They were just folks hanging out. That's all.
MARTIN: They weren't 'hanging out' like you—they're at college.
ALICE. And what made you come home, Danny? Have you come back for college?
DANNY: Nope.
MARTIN: Nope? Can you explain what you mean by 'nope'?
DANNY: No, Mother. I haven't come back to go to college.
ALICE: What will you do?

DANNY: I thought I might take up a sport again.

MARTIN: You're not a professional ball player, Dan. You don't have the ball skills. Stop wasting your time.

DANNY: No. Something else. Just something to give me discipline.

MARTIN: Since when have you been interested in discipline?

DANNY: Since now.

MARTIN: You weren't interested in discipline when you dropped out of college.

DANNY: No. I wasn't then. But I've changed.

ALICE: You can't earn money with sport.

DANNY: I've got a job, as a matter of fact.

ALICE: Where?

DANNY: I'm an orderly at the State Mental Hospital. I start this week.

ALICE: We know the head psychiatrist at the private hospital. We could talk to him about you getting a job there. It might be preferable.

DANNY: No, I'll stay there.

ALICE: Where are you living?

DANNY: Just in a little room in Trenton.

SAMMY: But you'll come to dinner sometimes, won't you, Danny?

SCENE EIGHTEEN

MARTY *is clearing up the table.* DANNY *is getting his stuff, ready to go.*

MARTY: I'm glad you're back, Danny.

DANNY: Thanks.

MARTY: Hey … Are you okay?

DANNY: Yeah. Yeah. I'm good.

MARTY: You seem different.

DANNY: I've just gotta get some discipline in my life. That's all.

MARTY: Well, I saw something. And it's funny—I thought of you when I saw it.

DANNY: What?

MARTY: Have you heard of *karate*?

DANNY: Japanese fighting?

MARTY: Yeah. Well, I was in Trenton and I saw one of their fighting places—called a *dojo* I think. There's a few of them opening up around the place. But this particular one happened to be in Trenton.

Where you live, would you believe? I watched through the windows.
They were beating the hell out of each other. But with discipline.

DANNY: Huh.

MARTY: I just thought, because you're in Trenton, it might be easy for
you to get to.

DANNY: Maybe.

MARTY: You need a lift back to Trenton tonight?

DANNY: You've got a car?

MARTY: I can borrow Mother's.

DANNY: Nah, I'll get the bus.

MARTY: I don't even have to tell her where we're going.

DANNY: Nah.

SCENE NINETEEN

DANNY *walks into the* karate dojo. *He passes* LOIS *as he walks in.*

DANNY: Excuse me—is this the *karate dojo*?

LOIS: It sure is.

DANNY: You go here?

LOIS: No, I'm dropping my brother off. You?

DANNY: My first day. I'm Danny.

LOIS: Hi, Danny. I'm Lois.

DANNY: You been around the *dojo* much?

LOIS: I haven't been around Trenton that much for a while. I was in
Mexico.

DANNY: Wow.

LOIS: I just got back a little while ago.

DANNY: How long were you there for?

LOIS: About a year. Just over.

DANNY: Living in Mexico—that's pretty cool. You actually left the US.

LOIS: Yeah.

DANNY: So you must like travelling.

LOIS: Sure. Yeah.

DANNY: That's a stupid thing to say, isn't it? Who doesn't like travelling?

LOIS: Well, some people don't like it at all. My sister Connie is happy
being here in New Jersey. She sees the whole world here. That's
lucky, I guess. To get to see the whole world in one little place.

DANNY: I lived in Kentucky. But that's not the same as Mexico.

LOIS: Wow—Kentucky sounds great!

DANNY: I didn't like it so much.

LOIS: Oh, well.

DANNY: But I'd still recommend it—I'd still recommend going and finding out for yourself.

LOIS: Okay. Well, thanks for the tip.

DANNY: What was the best thing about Mexico?

LOIS: Wow, that's a hard question. But overall, I'd say the Mexicans. They taught me a lot about how to live. I know that sounds silly, but they did.

DANNY: Like what?

LOIS: Well, for instance, say you asked me if I would lend you some money next week, something like a thousand dollars—even if I didn't have it and I didn't want to lend it. I'd just say yes. Because it's the polite thing to say and everyone's happy.

DANNY: But what happens next week when I come to get the money?

LOIS: I guess I just wouldn't answer the door. My friend and I—we learnt from that—just 'Yes 'em' we'd say. It makes most situations run pretty smoothly.

DANNY: Would you ever want to come for a meal or something with me? Maybe tomorrow? Or Saturday night? Do you like pizza?

LOIS: Oh—I'm really busy at the moment—I don't really want to date anyone because I'm hoping to join the Peace Corps again soon. So I'm sorry—

DANNY: I was just testing your theory. To see if you yes'd me.

LOIS: Oh, right! Ha ha!

> DANNY *pretends to laugh too.*

Well, I guess you better get to training. Apparently the Sensei gets real mad if people are late.

DANNY: Yeah. Well, um—

LOIS: Nice to meet you, Danny.

DANNY: You too, Lois.

> DANNY *goes into the dojo. Most of the people from the class are already there. They are cleaning the floor. Not really sure what to do, he joins them. The* SENSEI *watches them. One of the* GUYS

puts the floor cleaning cloth back on top of the others lopsided. The SENSEI *points to it, the* GUY *quickly straightens it.*

The class begins. They line up. DANNY *goes to the end of the line. He watches the others kneel down. He copies. They close their eyes.* DANNY*'s stay open, looking at the others. They begin a warm-up. Running, push-ups, sit-ups.*

Then they begin training. The SENSEI *leads. They begin doing punching and then adding kicks in.*

It is a powerful feeling. DANNY *is overwhelmed by it, but also a little left behind. He tries very hard.*

The SENSEI *leads the class. Straightening people, giving instructions.*

The SENSEI *adjusts them with a bamboo stick. He shows them exaggerated forms of what they are doing.*

SENSEI: Not like this. [*Raising his shoulders*] This. [*Easing his shoulders.*] Shouldn't come from shoulder. No power. Come from *hara*. From source.

He hits one GUY *in the stomach.*

Need to be firm. Come from *hara*.

DANNY *is doing his best to get stuff right.*

The SENSEI *approaches him, carrying the bamboo stick.*

The SENSEI *whacks him with the bamboo stick.*

Why you long hair? What you done should have long hair?

He whacks him again.

All throughout the class, the SENSEI *walks by* DANNY, *hitting him with the stick.*

The SENSEI *walks around him, looking him up and down.*

What is name?
DANNY: Danny.
SENSEI: Danny? Danny is child name.
DANNY: Or Dan.
SENSEI: I call you Danny. Why long hair, Danny?

He whacks him with the stick.

Many American want *karate*. Want to be black belt. But black belt is only white belt who never stop come. You think you get answer from *karate*. No answers. Just practise. Never stop. Practise every day. There is no answer. You understand?

DANNY: Yes.

SENSEI: You say '*oss*'.

DANNY: *Oss*.

SENSEI: You know what *oss* means?

DANNY: Yes?

SENSEI: Find out what *oss* means.

> *The* SENSEI *walks away.* DANNY *keeps his stance.* JERRY *comes over to him.*

JERRY: You were close. *Oss* means to push beyond the boundaries that you create. This is my boundary.

> *He holds up his club foot.*

DANNY: This is my boundary.

> *He hits himself on the head.* JERRY *laughs.*

JERRY: I'm Jerry.

DANNY: Danny.

JERRY: I got it. Child's name.

> *They laugh.*

You've got to deepen your stance. Front leg bent at the knee. Back leg straight. You've got to get right deep down.

DANNY: *Oss*.

END OF ACT ONE

ACT TWO

The hospital. DAN *and* PATTI *sit over* LOIS. PATTI *looks half asleep. But she's awake. She looks over at her grandfather.*

PATTI: Hospitals are so their own world.

DAN: I know what you mean.

PATTI: When you're not in one, you forget they exist. But the minute you step in one you feel yourself becoming part of the ecology. I spent a lot of time in hospitals. I got to know some of the regulars. And I got to hear all about their bladder infections.

> DAN *laughs.*

DAN: So many exciting things to look forward to.

PATTI: My bladder will be different.

DAN: That's what we all say.

PATTI: Do you ever wonder what you're doing on this side of the world?

DAN: No. Never.

PATTI: Imagine if we were all in America, in the hospital there. I wonder how different we would be.

DAN: Well, you probably wouldn't exist.

PATTI: Or maybe I would, but I would have been born into the right body. And maybe I'd have always just been your granddaughter.

DAN: There's no point thinking like that.

PATTI: I like it. It's like a really lame form of fantasy. Picturing your own life, but only slightly different. They made a movie about it. *Sliding Doors.* I think she dies in one of the versions. Isn't that sad? We could be in New Jersey and it could be the other way around, you in the bed and Grandma and me sitting and waiting.

DAN: The hospitals are better here.

PATTI: Maybe everything is just better now because it's forty-five years later.

SCENE TWO

DANNY *is at work at the mental hospital. One of the guards is there. It's time to shower the inmates.*

GUARD: Okay, you ready, Danny?
DANNY: Yeah.

> *One of the patients is screaming, naked.*

PATIENT: I don't want to! No! No!

> *The* GUARD *turns on the hose.* DANNY *sprays the* PATIENT *off, who screams.*

Why are you doing this to me?!
DANNY: I'm really sorry, buddy—but we have to, today's shower day.

> *He finishes spraying him off. The* MAN *from long ago—from the bar—comes. He smiles at* DANNY.

MAN: I'm dirty. All over.
DANNY: Okay, pal.

> DANNY *begins to spray him.*

MAN: How's your arm, son?

SCENE THREE

DANNY *is in the* dojo. *They're in the middle of training.* DANNY *is trying hard to learn the first kata, but he keeps getting mixed up. He is trying to copy the others and will sometimes almost get it, but then will mess something up.*

JERRY *is on a much more advanced kata, but his club foot keeps getting in his way. He is getting very frustrated with himself.*

The SENSEI *is moving around the class, adjusting everyone. He watches* DANNY.

SENSEI: Why you long hair?
DANNY: I don't know—I just haven't gotten it cut. Lots of guys have long hair now.
SENSEI: Long hair is not bad. Great men have long hair. Men who climb

tall mountain, men who save life of other. Men who do something great have long hair. What you done, Danny, to have long hair?

DANNY: Nothing.

SENSEI: Too high.

DANNY thinks that the SENSEI is referring to how he sees himself. He nods.

DANNY: *Oss*, Sensei.

DANNY bows. The SENSEI shakes his head.

SENSEI: Fix stance, Danny. Lower. Bend front knee. Lower.

The SENSEI adjusts DANNY with the stick, then moves on.

One of the BROWN BELTS begins to spar with JERRY. Because of his club foot, it is hard for JERRY to move fast enough out to escape the BROWN BELT's hits and kicks, and it is hard for him to move in fast enough to punch or kick the BROWN BELT. He also has trouble balancing on his club foot. The BROWN BELT is punching him too hard. JERRY tries to kick him, balancing on his club foot, but he falls down. The BROWN BELT jumps on top of him, doing fake elbows into him. One of them lands. DANNY runs and pulls the BROWN BELT off.

BROWN BELT: Hey!

DANNY stands back, ready to street-fight him.

You gonna fight me, tough guy?

The BROWN BELT goes to punch DANNY. DANNY blocks him. DANNY is not afraid.

The SENSEI notices.

SENSEI: Danny. One hundred push-ups.

DANNY: What— Why?

SENSEI: Two hundred push-ups.

DANNY: I was just stopping him from doing something that you should have stopped him doing.

SENSEI: Three hundred push-ups.

DANNY begrudgingly begins his push-ups. The SENSEI motions for the BROWN BELT to come spar. The SENSEI is going to test his spirit.

The rest of the class watches.

The SENSEI *is teaching the student, all of the students, and also going in quite hard.*

He kicks the BROWN BELT *in the head. The* BROWN BELT *falls down.*

No—not done.

The BROWN BELT *gets up. The* SENSEI *punches and slaps him. The* BROWN BELT *falls down again.*

Up. Not done.

The BROWN BELT *drags himself up. The* SENSEI *kicks him. The* BROWN BELT *falls.*

Not done. Up.

The BROWN BELT *says from the floor.*

BROWN BELT: I'm sorry, Sensei. I'm done.

SENSEI: You have no spirit.

The BROWN BELT *drags himself away.* JERRY *looks nervously at the* SENSEI *, wondering if the* SENSEI *is going to pick him to spar. But the* SENSEI *just pats* JERRY *on the arm. The* SENSEI *looks at* DANNY, *who is still doing the push-ups.*

You fight in the *dojo*, you fight *karate*. No street fight here. *Oss?*

DANNY: *Oss.*

SENSEI: You want *karate*?

DANNY: Yes.

SENSEI: You want to be *karateka*?

DANNY: Yes.

SENSEI: Man with honour have long hair. What have you done for honour? Why you long hair? Cut hair if you want to be *karateka*. [*To the class*] One hundred push-up. Everyone.

JERRY gets on the ground next to DANNY.

JERRY: What are you up to?

DANNY: Seventy. I'm screwed. You wanna grab a beer after training?

JERRY: Really?

DANNY: Of course. I'm gonna need it after this.

JERRY: Sure. Great.

SCENE FOUR

DANNY *and* JERRY *sit in Danny's apartment that has no furniture. They listen to the baseball on a beat-up, tiny radio. He has no chairs to sit on, they just sit on milk crates.* DANNY *eats beans from a tin, he passes* JERRY *a tin.*

JERRY: Thanks …

> *He has a bite of the beans.*

You a big baseball fan?
DANNY: Me? Sure. I guess.
JERRY: You ever play?
DANNY: A little. You?

> JERRY *laughs.*

JERRY: I tried. But me attempting to steal bases was pretty ridiculous. At least *karate*'s a solo thing, you know? I mean I belong to the club, and that's important to me—but at least I'm not letting a whole team down when I can't do something. How do you like *karate* so far?
DANNY: I don't know, man. I like it. But I'll be damned if I can remember any of the moves.
JERRY: Oh, that just takes a while. It took me six months to get my first *kata*. But you're strong. That's good.
DANNY: Hey, are you any good at haircuts?
JERRY: No way.
DANNY: You've gotta be better than me.

> *He grabs some scissors.*

Just do your best.

> JERRY *holds the scissors, uncertain.*

Though I wonder if I give in, if Sensei will lose respect for me …
JERRY: I don't know if that's the way Sensei sees it …

> *A knock on his door. It's* MARTIN.

DANNY: Hello, Father. What are you doing here?
MARTIN: I had to come into Trenton and run some errands.
DANNY: This is my friend Jerry.

> MARTIN *nods at* JERRY.

MARTIN: Your mother said you've been doing *karate*.

DANNY: That's right.

MARTIN: I fought against the Japanese in the war.

DANNY: I know, Father. But that was a long time ago.

MARTIN: Tell that to my fellow soldiers who didn't come back. Did you hear about the Strong boys?

DANNY: No.

MARTIN: Robert was conscripted to fight in Vietnam and his two brothers are joining him. They enlisted. They're going to serve our country.

DANNY: All three of them. That's a real shame.

MARTIN: I served this country. I fought the Japanese and the Nazis on behalf of this country. You've shown you have no respect for me, your father. But what about your country?

DANNY: Father, I have a friend over.

MARTIN: [*to* JERRY] You thinking of enlisting, son?

JERRY: No, sir. They won't take me because of my foot.

MARTIN: They probably wouldn't take Danny anyway because of his arm.

JERRY: You've got an arm injury, Danny?

MARTIN *looks to the radio.*

MARTIN: Good game.

DANNY: Yeah.

MARTIN: How is your arm feeling?

DANNY: I don't really think about it anymore.

MARTIN: I don't think there was ever anything wrong with your arm. I don't think it went dead. I think you just pitched a bad game. And were afraid you'd pitch more bad games. You psyched yourself out. That's the difference between you and anyone who's ever stuck to something. That's the difference between you and the Strong boys. You're a bad example to your brothers.

DANNY *screams at him.*

DANNY: Shut the hell up!

MARTIN: What did you say to me?

DANNY: I said shut up—shut the hell up! Whoever said I wanted to be an example to anybody?!

MARTIN: You can't just pick and choose your responsibilities in this life. I never thought my son would grow up to be a man I'm ashamed of.

MARTIN *leaves.*

JERRY: I'll give it a try.
DANNY: What?
JERRY: Your haircut.
DANNY: Nah, forget it. I'll keep it long.

SCENE FIVE

DAN *is sitting over* LOIS. PATTI *isn't there. She comes back in, with all of her long hair cut off, jaggedly.*

PATTI: It took me so long to grow my hair. I can't even tell you. I loved it. I loved having long hair. I think that was the thing that made me feel most like myself. More than breasts might. More than a vagina would. Way more than make-up or clothes. It was my hair. I knew, as soon as he left me, I knew I was going to cut it off. And then I just did it. It's in the trash in the hospital toilets. And it was virgin hair, never been died. I could have at least sold it to make a wig. God knows I need the rent money.
DAN: I can lend you money, Patti.
PATTI: I just cut my hair off. I lost the man I love and I cut my hair off.
DAN: Patti, I just can't right now. I just can't buy into the drama right now. I'm sorry.
PATTI: What the hell am I doing here? I shouldn't have brought my problems in here. I should go. I was just— I'm scared. Sorry, Grandad. I'm sorry I bothered you with all this while Grandma's sick.

> PATTI *grabs her bag. She is going.*

DAN: Wait, Patti.

> PATTI *stops.*

You don't have to go.
PATTI: My heart hurts.

SCENE SIX

Back in the dojo. *Training. Everyone's filing in. Getting ready. Warming up. They do the clean-up on the floors, and then line up. The* SENSEI *walks by* DANNY.

DANNY *bows. This time, the* SENSEI *bows back.*

SENSEI: Again spirit training. You, Danny. I test spirit.

> DANNY *steps forward. He stands facing the* SENSEI. *Ready to spar. They bow. They begin.* DANNY *is full of energy. Jumping around. The* SENSEI *roundhouse kicks him in the face.* DANNY *lurches back, but doesn't fall.*

> *They move around each other.* DANNY *goes to punch, the* SENSEI *blocks him, punches him.* DANNY *falls back, but catches himself. The* SENSEI *lets* DANNY *right himself, then kicks him.* DANNY *stumbles to the ground, but quickly gets up. He comes at the* SENSEI, *but the* SENSEI *easily moves out the way.*

> *The* SENSEI *chops* DANNY *in the chest. Then kicks him across the stomach.* DANNY *falls to the ground. Quickly gets up.*

> *The* SENSEI *kicks him again.* DANNY *stumbles, but doesn't fall.*

> *The* SENSEI *roundhouse kicks* DANNY *in the head.* DANNY *falls to the ground. He is knocked out for a minute. He wakes up. Gets up. Bows. He is unsteady on his feet.*

Not done. Keep fighting, Danny.

> DANNY *bows again.*

You land one good punch, kick, we finish.

> DANNY *bows again. They begin again. They go into a rally of sorts, punching, kicking, blocking, then* DANNY *lands one. He lands a kick on the* SENSEI. *They stop.*

I think you got spirit, Danny. Now see I am right. But you have not earned honour. Cut hair.

> *They bow to each other.*

> *Training finishes.* JERRY *helps the* SENSEI *take things into the back office. It is just* DANNY *in the* dojo. LOIS *walks into the* dojo, *cautiously.* DANNY *sees her.*

DANNY: Hi. Lois. You're back.

LOIS: Hi. I'm meeting my brother Jerry. Is he here?

DANNY: Oh, yeah, he's just in the back office with Sensei.

LOIS: Oh, great.

DANNY: Do you want me to let him know you're here?

LOIS: Oh, that's okay, it's not a rush. I can just wait.

DANNY: You know, Jerry's told me lots of stories about you and your sister Connie. Sounds like the two of you are wild!

LOIS: Oh, no—that's Connie! She's the wild one!

DANNY: Yeah, well, sounds like you guys all have a ball.

LOIS: Do you have brothers and sisters?

DANNY: Two brothers.

LOIS: I'll bet you guys have good times.

DANNY: Sure.

LOIS: How are you doing at *karate* so far?

DANNY: I'm terrible. But I love it.

LOIS: You're all the same. Jerry thinks he's terrible too. But Jerry thinks he's terrible at everything. I'll bet you're both great though.

DANNY: Great's a strong word. But we're definitely trying.

LOIS: It looks like dancing to me.

DANNY: Dancing?

LOIS: All those moves. And the poise. It's like ballet.

DANNY: Well, that explains why I'm so bad at it. I'm a terrible dancer. I'll bet you're good though.

LOIS: I'm okay.

DANNY: That means you're good.

LOIS: I'm probably better than you and Jerry. But that doesn't make me good.

DANNY: You should start up *karate*, start coming to the *dojo*.

LOIS: Oh, I don't like violence.

DANNY: But in *karate* you're just reacting if someone attacks you— you don't instigate.

LOIS: It's too much responsibility to fight back then if someone attacks me. I'd rather just play dead.

DANNY *laughs.*

DANNY: So forget *karate*.

LOIS: I do like those chops though. If I could learn one thing, it would be how to *karate* chop.

DANNY: I could teach you.

LOIS: But you just said you were terrible!

DANNY: Not terrible …

> LOIS *laughs.*

> *He smiles at her.*

> JERRY *comes out. The* SENSEI *watches them from the doorway of the back office.*

JERRY: Hey, Lo Lo! Where's Con?
LOIS: She waited in the car.
JERRY: She is so lazy!

> CONNIE *enters.*

CONNIE: I'm here!
JERRY: Meet my sisters, Connie—
CONNIE: Charmed I'm sure.
JERRY: And Lois.
DANNY & LOIS: [*together*] We met.

> *They laugh.*

CONNIE: [*to* DANNY] Don't you have a name?
DANNY: I'm Danny. Good to meet you.
CONNIE: Ha ha! Listen to him, 'Danny. Good to meet you.' Is he a card or what? 'Danny. Good to meet you.'

> DANNY *laughs.*

You guys sure spend a lot of time in this wooden room.
JERRY: Danny practically lives here. He's a crazy man.
DANNY: Nah, I've just got a lot to learn. Jerry said you're both trained as teachers. You must really know stuff.
JERRY: Are you kidding? My sisters know stuff? No way.
CONNIE: Two plus two is four! Screw you, Jerry!

> *She grabs him in a bear hug.* JERRY *laughs, but tries to squirm away.*

Oh, what a little cutie!
JERRY: Careful, Connie—I've got *karate* instincts now.

> *He lifts his hand to a chopping position.*

CONNIE: My little itty-bitty brother would never *karate* chop his big sissie.

JERRY: Not on purpose—but it's my reflexes you oughta be worried about!

She wraps him harder in the bear hug.

CONNIE: Chop your way outta this, Jerry Pooh!

JERRY: Enough, Con.

DANNY *speaks to* LOIS.

DANNY: Looks like you need *karate* in your family.

LOIS *laughs.*

CONNIE: Me and Lois hate exercise. Lucky we're born skinny. Fish-stick Michlik they called us both in high school. Of course Lois got the name first 'cause she's three years older.

DANNY: Really?

LOIS: No! That's Connie's favourite gag—saying I'm her older sister! It's the other way around!

JERRY: Nobody ever falls for it anyway.

CONNIE: Hey!

LOIS: Okay—time to go, gang.

CONNIE: We're going to the Candlelight Bar—you with us or against, Danny?

DANNY: I'm with you.

SCENE SEVEN

Out on the frozen New Jersey River, DANNY *and the others practise their katas in bare feet and bare-chested. The* SENSEI *walks on the ice, showing no sign of feeling the cold.*

JERRY: Man, special winter training sounded fun. This isn't fun. Who runs on ice? Two words. Frost. Bite. We're going to lose our toes. But, Danny, you look like you're having fun. How come you're having fun?

JERRY *is working very hard too, but still is having trouble, especially on the ice.*

DANNY *is in a zone. He is not feeling the cold. His* karate *is improving. He is moving swiftly and smoothly.*

Later that night, they are sleeping in sleeping bags in the dojo. *The wind is coming in through the cracks in the windows—it's freezing.* DANNY *sneaks out a bottle of bourbon. He takes a swig.*

DANNY: Hey, Jerry, have some of this bourbon. It will warm you up.

He hands JERRY *the bourbon.*

JERRY: Aren't you scared of Sensei?
DANNY: Of course.

JERRY *shrugs and has a sip. He coughs.*

JERRY: Sorry.
DANNY: It's strong and cheap. The second one'll taste better.

JERRY *looks unsure, but has another sip. He hands the bottle back to* DANNY.

Hey, what happened with that girl at your work you like? You ask her out yet?
JERRY: Nah. I don't want to embarrass her. You know, make it awkward for her at work.
DANNY: You can't think like that, man. You gotta have some confidence. Worst that happens is she says no. But why would she? You're a handsome guy.
JERRY: I don't know. I just … I just always put it down to my foot, you know. Like when I think of myself, it's all I see. And I think that's what she'd see.
DANNY: That's stupid, Jerry. You're a whole lot more than your foot.
JERRY: Well, maybe if I make it to green belt, then I'll ask her out. I might see myself real different if I make it to green belt.

They fall asleep.

As though no time has gone by, it's dawn and time for training. They all get up and train hard, until it's time for everyone to start leaving for work.

SCENE EIGHT

JERRY *and* DANNY *walk into the Michlik house. Drunk. They tip-toe—it's very late at night.* DANNY *walks into something.*

DANNY: [*whispering*] Sorry!

JERRY: I knew you'd bump into something. Usually it's me. Michliks are renowned heavy sleepers anyway. My father snores too loud to hear anything else and my mother's going deaf from being blasted by it every night. And Connie—nothing wakes her up—we couldn't wake her up if we brought in a brass band— All of them heavy sleepers—except—

LOIS *comes walking out, in her nightgown.*

For Lois.

DANNY: Hi, Lois.

LOIS: Hi, Danny.

DANNY: Sorry we woke you up, Lois.

LOIS: You didn't. I heard you guys and got up to see if you were hungry. I feel like making a tuna casserole.

DANNY: Are you kidding? I'm starved!

LOIS: How about you, Jerry?

JERRY: I've always got room for your tuna casserole.

LOIS *starts to cook.* DANNY *sits. He's drunk, but keeps upright, polite.* JERRY *sits down and is soon sound asleep.*

LOIS: You boys been drinking?

DANNY: Yeah. With Sensei.

LOIS: I don't know how you drink until so late and then get up so early in the morning. I couldn't do it. I could do the drinking. But not the getting up and punching the wall part.

DANNY: The punching the wall part is easy. It's the drinking that's hard.

LOIS: Do you like a lotta tuna in a casserole?

DANNY: Oh, yeah. Definitely. I love tuna.

LOIS: Me too. I make either this one or an eggplant casserole. They're my two favourites. I like the eggplant one the best, but everyone else likes the tuna.

DANNY: Oh—I love eggplant.

LOIS: Some people are allergic to it. Isn't that funny? It's poison to some people.

DANNY: Well, yeah, everything's allergic to at least something. Even tuna, probably. But not me, I'm not allergic to anything.

LOIS: That's lucky. Unless you are, but you're still yet to come across it.

DANNY: I hope not. I do get a leg cramp from red wine sometimes.

LOIS: Well, that sounds a bit like an allergy.

DANNY: Great—so I do have one! What about you, Lois? What are you allergic to?

LOIS: Oak trees.

DANNY: No!

LOIS: It's true. Every spring I get so allergic to their pollen. They kill me. But I get allergic to things pretty easy. I've sort of got a weak constitution. Not like you.

DANNY: Oh, everybody's got different strengths.

LOIS: I guess I've got pretty good eyesight.

DANNY: Oh, I've got terrible eyesight! Real terrible!

LOIS: Well then, you can stand oak trees, but I can see their leaves better. Fair's fair.

DANNY: Fair's fair. Will you look at that?

LOIS: What?

DANNY: Jerry? Stone cold out.

LOIS: Oh, Jerry falls asleep wherever he sits. You wouldn't think so—because he can be pretty tense. Always has been. But when it comes to sleep—he just goes. My whole family—deep—

DANNY: Sleepers.

> LOIS *does something with the casserole. Maybe it's ready for the oven.*

What about you? Did you go somewhere tonight?

LOIS: Yeah, I went to the White Horse Bowling Alley. You ever been there?

DANNY: Sure. But not for years. Fun there?

LOIS: Yeah—but I'm a terrible bowler!

DANNY: Even with your good eyesight—

LOIS: I can see the pins, but I'll be damned if I can throw that thing straight.

DANNY: If we could use your eyes and my arms to roll the ball, I'll bet we'd score pretty high.

LOIS: Ha ha! That's a funny image. I can just see my eyes, but real big and googly—not in my head or anything—and your arms—but that's it—not one other limb—no legs—no head—only eyes and arms!

DANNY: That is funny! Who'd you go bowling with tonight?

LOIS: Oh, some friends of mine—and Connie too. She's pretty good actually. She came fourth.

DANNY: How many of you were there?

LOIS: Five.

> JERRY *wakes up.*

JERRY: I'm starving. I think I'm drunk.

LOIS: I better get back to the casserole.

JERRY: Who wants to play cards? Danny?

DANNY: Sure thing.

JERRY: Rummy? How about rummy?

DANNY: You got it.

> JERRY *gets a deck of cards.*

JERRY: I'll shuffle. Actually maybe you better shuffle.

> DANNY *begins to shuffle.*

Lois is a good person. A very good person.

DANNY: She sure is.

LOIS: Well, that's nice of both of you. But I think I put too much celery in the casserole.

> *She watches* DANNY *and* JERRY *playing cards. She whispers to* DANNY:

Thank you.

DANNY: What for? I love rummy.

> LOIS *laughs.*

Hey, Lois, are you good at cutting hair?

JERRY: She's the best in our family.

LOIS: That's not saying much.

DANNY: Would you cut my hair?

LOIS: Right now?

DANNY: Yeah. I wanna surprise Sensei tomorrow.

LOIS: Well, okay … But it'll mean the casserole will take longer.

DANNY: I'm in no rush.

LOIS: But Jerry's starving.

JERRY: I'm not as hungry as Danny's hair is long.

> LOIS *takes some scissors and begins to carefully cut* DANNY's *hair.*

SCENE NINE

DANNY *and* JERRY *come into the* dojo. *The* SENSEI *sees* DANNY*'s haircut.*
DANNY *bows to the* SENSEI.

DANNY: *Oss*, Sensei.
SENSEI: *Oss*, Danny.
DANNY: What do you think of my hair, Sensei?
SENSEI: Very bad. Very ugly. But not so ugly as before.

> DANNY *realises that the* SENSEI *is joking with him.* DANNY *laughs.*
> *The* SENSEI *gives him a stern look.*

Line up!

> *They all run into a line.*

Grading is coming up. These are the students nominate to grade.
Danny and Jerry.

> JERRY *gives* DANNY *an excited, but nervous look.*

SCENE TEN

DAN *and* PATTI *sit in the hospital room. Totally quiet. Patti's phone begins
to ring.* PATTI *looks at it and jumps.*

PATTI: It's him! It's Rex, Grandad.
DAN: You can answer it if you want.
PATTI: No—we're in the hospital— Really?
DAN: If you want.

> PATTI *answers it.*

PATTI: [*on the phone*] Hello? [*She listens.*] I'm in the hospital actually.
[*Listens.*] No, I'm fine. I'm here with my grandparents.

> *She gets up and stands outside the doorway.*

I told you. My Grandma. Well, of course we're close. They raised
me mostly because my mother was a teenage tramp when I was born.
[*Listens.*] Very funny. [*Her voice changes.*] I'm so glad you called.
[*Listens.*] Oh. I don't know. How do you expect me to know? [*Listens.*]
Check the hall cupboard and if it's not there check the cupboard in the
study where the other board games are.

DAN *is listening to the conversation.*

Who are you going to play it with? [*Listens.*] So you're calling me to see if I know where it is, but you're not inviting me to play. [*Listens.*] I never moved your stuff around—only to make things neater and you liked it. [*Listens.*] Well, it seemed to me like you liked it. That's why I did it. Because I was trying to be helpful to you. [*Listens.*] Okay. Cool. Well, have fun playing Settlers of Catan. By the way, I have a haircut.

> *She listens. By* PATTI*'s face, it is obvious Rex is not interested in her haircut.*

Goodbye.

> PATTI *hangs up. She stands in the doorway for a moment. She gulps in a cry.*

DAN: Are you okay, Patti?

PATTI: Yes, Grandad. I'm good. It's good to see the truth.

DAN: The truth changes. Remember that.

PATTI: What we want the truth to be changes. How we fool ourselves changes.

DAN: Maybe you don't fool yourself. Maybe you're the opposite. Too hard on yourself.

PATTI: No, Grandad. I know what I am. You know too. I don't belong anywhere. I don't belong here. I'm just making everything worse. I didn't belong with Rex. And now my hair's fucked up as a woman. There's nowhere for me. And my saying that to you is the worst thing— Who does this—who comes by their grandmother's deathbed and talks about wanting to die?

DAN: You know what I was like when I was your age? I was a mess.

PATTI: But you had the *dojo*. The past made more sense than now.

SCENE ELEVEN

DANNY *is walking along the street, towards the* dojo. *He runs into* LOIS.

LOIS: Hi, Danny!

DANNY: Hi.

LOIS: I just dropped Jerry off. Are you doing anything later? After training?

DANNY: Nothing—I'm not doing anything.

LOIS: Oh, great! Because I've got some good news!

DANNY: What is it?

LOIS: I've got a placement with the Peace Crops in Kansas.

DANNY: Wow.

LOIS: I'm going in a week.

DANNY: That's wonderful.

LOIS: So maybe we can all go out tonight to celebrate?

> DANNY's *heart sinks. All he can manage is a weak smile.*

DANNY: Actually I'm a little tired right now. I didn't realise.

LOIS: Are you okay?

DANNY: Sure. Just tired.

LOIS: Okay.

DANNY: Yeah. Just tired.

LOIS: You don't look like yourself.

DANNY: No. I do. That's the problem. I'll see you later, Lois.

> *He heads off.*

LOIS: Well, hope you have a good … rest.

> LOIS *leaves.*

DANNY: Lois, wait—

> *She doesn't hear him.*

SCENE TWELVE

YOUNG DANNY *walks into the* dojo. *In the hospital room,* OLD DAN *stands up.* PATTI *is crying.*

The SENSEI *is in the* dojo.

SENSEI: Danny. In time of sorrow, need to put body to pain. To lift heart. Time punch *makiwara* boards now.

> YOUNG DANNY *begins to punch the boards.* OLD DAN *begins to punch.* PATTI *stands outside the hospital room and hits her phone into the wall, crying.*

Yes. Knuckles bleed. Blood is good tears. Open the heart. Good.

> DANNY *punches and punches the boards, blood flying from his*

knuckles. JERRY *punches the makiwara boards too. Pelting them like a child having a tantrum—he hits them, hurting his own hands, hitting the boards, ineffectually, in a flurry of fists.*

DANNY *and* OLD DAN, *side-by-side in different worlds. Both of them grieving over* LOIS. PATTI *looks in the mirror. She punches herself in the face.*

The SENSEI *begins to sing. They silently punch as the* SENSEI *sings. The worlds have merged for a moment.*

DANNY *finally stands, his knuckles a bloody mess.* JERRY *continues pelting the boards.*

The MAN *with the dead arm walks into the* dojo. *He looks at* DANNY.

MAN: You don't really think you can be part of the world, do you, son? You don't really think there's a place for a screw-up like you, do you? Your ideas were big. But you scrambled everything. I told you— never take LSD. Fuck America. Only way out of this country is via the grave.

The MAN *leaves the* dojo.

JERRY *approaches* DANNY.

JERRY: Hey, Danny, sorry to bother you, but can you spar with me? I don't think I'm gonna be ready for grading. I don't think I'm gonna be able to do it— The kicks where I have to balance on … my … in front of the whole class— I don't want to let Sensei down— I don't know why he picked me—I'm not green belt material—

DANNY: You mind if we raincheck, Jerry?

JERRY: Sure … Of course …

DANNY: You'll be fine.

JERRY: Yeah …

DANNY: I'm sure you'll get it.

JERRY: I don't think I will, Danny.

DANNY: It's just a belt.

JERRY: Yeah. I guess.

DANNY: I'm gonna go. I'll see you at Lois's thing.

DANNY *leaves.*

As JERRY *leaves the* dojo, *the* BROWN BELT *from before is finishing up training.* JERRY *seems to be having some sort of anxiety attack. He looks through his bag.*

BROWN BELT: You okay, Jerry?

JERRY: Pardon?

BROWN BELT: You okay?

JERRY: Fine. Fine.

The BROWN BELT *turns away and goes back to his kata. Once he's turned,* JERRY *finds a pill in his bag, swallows it. The* BROWN BELT *turns back to him.* JERRY *looks at him.*

Can I ask you something?

BROWN BELT: Sure.

JERRY: You'll tell me the truth?

BROWN BELT: Yup. Try to.

JERRY: Is the only reason that people help me here because they feel sorry for me? Or do they really think I can get better?

BROWN BELT: You know what Sensei's like. All about spirit, blah, blah, *oss*. Don't put limitations on yourself. But some people are born with limitations. Like you. So maybe you could give yourself a break, you know?

JERRY: A break …

BROWN BELT: *Karate*'s not going to help you, Jerry. And you're wasting your time and everybody else's when you keep coming. I'm sorry. But you asked me to be honest.

JERRY: I appreciate it.

The BROWN BELT *exits.*

JERRY, *alone, does his kata. For the first time, calmly. He finishes. He bows. He zips up his bag. Picks it up. He bows.*

SCENE THIRTEEN

DANNY, LOIS *and* CONNIE *are drinking. It is a going-away party. They are having shots. The* SENSEI *is there and others too.* JERRY *is not there.*

CONNIE: Hey, where the heck is Jerry?

DANNY: He was still at the *dojo* when I left.

CONNIE: He better hurry up or he'll miss everything. Like my speech!

She stands up.

To my little sissie who's going all the way by her little self to Kansas.

THE OTHERS: To Lois.

CONNIE: May she not be killed by a tornado!

LOIS: I second that!

CONNIE: May she come back soon so we don't die of broken hearts!

DANNY: Cheers.

CONNIE: May she not fall in love and get married in Kansas and raise a bunch of yokels!

THE OTHERS: Cheers.

CONNIE: No yokels! No yokels! Everybody, now! No yokels! No yokels! No yokels!

> DANNY *joins in the chant*—LOIS *does too—laughing and laughing.*

ALL: No yokels! No yokels! No yokels! No yokels!

> LOIS *gets up, laughing.* DANNY *follows her. They stand alone.*

DANNY: You know what's funny?

LOIS: What?

DANNY: You're going to Kansas and it starts with a K. I went to Kentucky and it starts with a K. Before I knew you.

LOIS: That's kind of funny.

DANNY: It's not that funny, is it?

LOIS: No. It's a pretty long bow.

DANNY: You know, Lois—when you get back from Kansas maybe—

LOIS: Danny—

DANNY: Please. Hear me out. When you get back from Kansas, maybe we could go out sometimes, just the two of us—I don't know—spend some more time together more—I don't know—

LOIS: Danny, I think you're the greatest. But I told you, I want to be friends.

DANNY: Yeah. I know. Worth a shot though, huh?

LOIS: Our friendship is real important to me, Danny.

DANNY: Yeah, of course. I'm really glad about that. It means a real lot to me.

LOIS: So don't be sad. Friends is better anyway. It lasts forever. What's the other? Just a couple weeks, months if we're lucky? I'm going to Kansas anyhow, Danny.

DANNY: Yeah. I know.

LOIS: With a K, like Kentucky.
DANNY: I guess it is a pretty small coincidence.
LOIS: Yeah, but who's counting.

> DANNY *kisses her. She kisses him back. But then she pulls away.*

I gotta pee real bad.

> LOIS *slips out.* DANNY *says to himself, at the same time as* OLD
> DAN *says in the hospital:*

DANNY & OLD DAN: [*together*] Don't go.

SCENE FOURTEEN

CONNIE *and* LOIS *and* DANNY *arrive home.*

LOIS: You want some meatloaf for the road, Danny?
DANNY: Yeah, I'll come say hi to Jerry. I feel bad leaving him at the *dojo*.
CONNIE: Jer-Jer! We're home! You missed the party!

> *The lights turn on.* JERRY *is hanging from the ceiling. His club foot
> swings beneath him.*

SCENE FIFTEEN

A new night in the dojo. *The* SENSEI *is sitting alone, drinking sake.*

SENSEI: Sit down, Danny.

> DANNY *sits down.*

I come to America from Japan. Like dandelion seed, we blow. As
karate man. I come to America, show *karate*. And when I come here,
already, many man lost. Many man, looking for *karate*. American
man lost. When you come, Danny, lost.
DANNY: *Oss*, Sensei.
SENSEI: But you, Danny, walk long way. Forest. Mountains. Ocean. You
got here, Danny. You now yourself. Strong feet, Danny.
DANNY: *Oss*.
SENSEI: Good, you know that.
DANNY: *Oss*.
SENSEI: But Jerry—Jerry—foot so weak. Not strong. Jerry, smart head,
sad chest, weak fist, dead feet. You see, Danny, I come to America.

My country lose war. Everyone suicide. If we lose war to America, people think, Japan bad. America good. Better we are America than Japan. But some know. Some wise know. Better we are Japan. Keep Japanese way, keep tradition, keep honour, we must go outside. So to spread Japan, I come to America. Teach Japanese way. Teach *karate*. If Japan suicide to be America, then make America Japan. But Jerry, what he has done is not Japanese way. He give up. There is no honour in that. I try to help him. To honour himself. But he kill himself for shame. I come to America. What for? *Dojo*—what for?

DANNY: You tried to help him, Sensei. None of us knew—how much … how much he hated himself.

SENSEI: Hate self world over. *Karate* should—*karate* should—

DANNY: It did. For me.

SENSEI: No. You just got strong feet, Danny.

DANNY: Now I do. But not before. I hated myself. Like Jerry. I wanted to die. But you made me have honour.

SENSEI: Before I saw you tonight I think I close *dojo*. Close *dojo* for honour. For honour of Japan. For honour of America. For honour of Jerry.

DANNY: I think the *dojo* should stay open, Sensei. For honour.

SENSEI: Smart, Danny. Maybe one day you have long hair.

DANNY: It's too late, Sensei. I'm starting to go bald. Every time I comb it, it comes out.

SENSEI: That is honour too.

DANNY: Really?

SENSEI: No. Not really.

> *The* SENSEI *hands* DANNY *a shot.*

Drink, Danny. Then we train.

> *They drink together.*

SCENE SIXTEEN

The SENSEI *leads them in a Japanese death ceremony. Everyone is there. It finishes.*

LOIS *comes up to* DANNY.

LOIS: Thanks for everything you did for Jerry.

DANNY: He was my friend. I should have done more.

LOIS: He left a suicide note. That he'd written ten years ago.

DANNY: Wow.

LOIS: So this wasn't new. I'm not mad at him. If the world was too hard, then the world was too hard. It is for some people. And you wish they'd wait. You wish they'd jump over the hump and see what's next. Because there usually is something next.

DANNY: Yeah.

LOIS: So I'm really going to Kansas now. Well, not this second. But I won't see you before I go.

DANNY: Well, okay.

> The BROWN BELT *from before comes up to* LOIS.

BROWN BELT: I'm so sorry about your brother.

LOIS: Thank you.

> The BROWN BELT *rushes off, his head hung.* LOIS *turns to* DANNY.

I never told you. One time when I came into the *dojo*, you were all training with no shirts. And I saw this guy from behind and I thought, what a beautiful back that man has. And then he turned around, and it was you. And I knew then, that I was in love with you.

DANNY: What?

LOIS: But I'm not ready.

DANNY: I can wait.

LOIS: I saw a wedding dress for sale. I bought it. It was cheap. It's just a real simple dress. I'll just keep it in my trunk of my car like I have been. I'll just keep it there until I come back.

> *She leaves.*

SCENE SEVENTEEN

Time has passed. YOUNG DANNY *is a black belt now. He's practising in the* dojo, *alone.*

In the hospital, OLD DAN *finds* PATTI *in the bathroom, punching herself in the face. He grabs her hands and stops her. She is half unconscious.*

OLD DAN: I don't know what to do. I don't know how to help you, Patti. I didn't know how to help your Uncle Jerry. I don't know how to help Lois. And I don't know how to help you.

PATTI *begins to sing. To sort of dance. It becomes apparent that she is singing 'Land' from the 'Horses' album by Patti Smith. The song becomes bigger and bigger. It begins to take over the whole world. It takes over the hospital. It takes over the* dojo.

And then, suddenly, PATTI *is inside the* dojo. *Her face bleeding. She looks around.*

PATTI: I know where I am. I'm in the *dojo*.

Back in the hospital, OLD DAN *is calling out to her.*

OLD DAN: Patti?! Patti?!

PATTI *walks through the* dojo, *still half dancing to 'Land'.*

YOUNG DANNY *sees her. He comes over.*

DANNY: Can I help you?
PATTI: How do you like that? I'm finally here.
DANNY: Have you been thinking about starting *karate* for a while?
PATTI: Oh, no. Not me!
DANNY: We've got a lot of women in the club. You'd fit right in.
PATTI: I don't know. I'm more into rock-and-roll.

She looks closer at him.

Hey, I know you. It's you.
DANNY: Dan.
PATTI: Yeah. You're so young. You're younger than me.
DANNY: Sorry. I've got a really bad memory for faces.
PATTI: That's okay.
DANNY: But you do look familiar.

He looks at her bruised face.

You get in a fight or something?
PATTI: Just with myself.
DANNY: Toughest opponent.
PATTI: You can say that again.
DANNY: I'm running the training today. Why don't you stay?
PATTI: You're a black belt. That's really impressive.
DANNY: You could be a black belt.
PATTI: Are you kidding?
DANNY: You know how someone becomes a black belt?

PATTI: How?

DANNY: They're a white belt that never stops coming.

PATTI: Oh, yeah? That's cool.

DANNY: You are what you do every day. That's life. That's the secret. You are what you practise. Nothing more. Nothing less. You don't need to know the answers. Just keep going. Keep working every day.

PATTI: That's pretty cool. I'll remember that. You'll have to as well. When times get harder.

DANNY: I'll try to.

PATTI: What year is it?

DANNY: 1977.

PATTI: You'll get married this year.

DANNY: Nah. The only woman I've ever loved is gone.

> OLD DAN *appears with them. He is doing the same kata as* YOUNG DANNY. *The sound of* LOIS*'s voice:*

LOIS: Danny? Danny?

DANNY: Lois?

OLD DAN: Lois?

PATTI: She's back here. In the *dojo*.

DANNY & OLD DAN: [*together*] Lois.

> *In the hospital room. Just* PATTI *and* OLD DAN. *Standing over the bed.* OLD DAN *leans over the bed and weeps.*

PATTI: We're gonna be okay, Grandad. You and me. We're gonna be okay.

THE END

Belvoir and Stuck Pigs Squealing present

BACK AT THE DOJO

By **LALLY KATZ**
Director **CHRIS KOHN**

This production of Back at the Dojo *opened at Belvoir St Theatre on Wednesday 22 June 2016.*

Set & Costume Designer **MEL PAGE**
Lighting Designer **RICHARD VABRE**
Composer & Sound Designer **JETHRO WOODWARD**
Dramaturgs **LOUISE GOUGH**
& ANTHEA WILLIAMS
Karate Consultant **NATSUKO MINEGHISHI**
Consultant **TRANSGENDER VICTORIA**
Producer Stuck Pigs Squealing **NINA BONACCI**
Voice Coach **SUZANNE HEYWOOD**
Stage Manager **MEL DYER**
Assistant Stage Manager **KEIREN SMITH**
Assistant Stage Manager (first week of rehearsals)
LYNDIE LI WAN PO
Directorial Secondment **OLIVIA SATCHELL**

With
FAYSSAL BAZZI
DARA CLEAR
CATHERINE DAVIES
HARRY GREENWOOD
BRIAN LIPSON
NATSUKO MINEGHISHI
LUKE MULLINS
SHARI SEBBENS

Back at the Dojo was commissioned by
Stuck Pigs Squealing, with funding support
from the Australia Council for the Arts and
Creative Victoria.

The development of this project has been
assisted by the Australian Government
through the Australia Council, its arts
funding and advisory body.

Back at the Dojo was developed in the
CultureLAB with the assistance of the
City of Melbourne through Arts House.

PHOTOGRAPHY Pia Johnson
DESIGN Alphabet Studio

Harry Greenwood

WRITER'S NOTE

Lally Katz

I grew up hearing stories of my father's twenties in a karate dojo in Trenton, New Jersey. This karate dojo has always been a mystical place within my family. It has become part of our family mythology how my father lost his mind on drugs and how the hard-ass sensei at the dojo helped him to recover his mind through the discipline of the body. My father met my mother through the karate dojo. In 2010, I brought the idea to do a play inspired by this to my longtime collaborator, director Chris Kohn. He was immediately drawn to doing a karate play and brought in Sensei Natsuko Mineghishi (who would become my sensei – though I'm only a yellow belt and have been demoted back to white).

In 2010, I also met a young woman on a bus in Australia. She had a New York accent and I told her I was born in New Jersey. I felt the same magic dust sprinkling feeling that I'd felt the first time I met Anna in *Neighbourhood Watch* and a handful of other women that I became obsessed with and wrote about. She and I exchanged phone numbers and met up. She told me that she had always been a woman, but had been born a man biologically and was now beginning transition. We hung out another few times and then I went overseas for five months and eventually lost touch. But as I started writing *Back at the Dojo* later that year, I found her story working its way into the telling of the story of the dojo.

Although the play started off being about my father and originally was going to have him in it playing himself (but we had to fire him because he wasn't believable enough), it has become something else. This isn't my dad's life. These are stories inspired by my dad's life and character. But I really took creative license and made up a lot of stuff about him that simply was never true. He's taken this pretty well on the whole.

Most of my plays are a mixture of true stories and people from my life mixed with made up stories and dreams. Sometimes people get really mad at me for this. Sometimes when the character is myself, I get really mad at me for this too.

Both Belvoir and Stuck Pigs have been homes to many of these plays. Belvoir commissioned and produced *Neighbourhood Watch* (a partially true, partially made-up story about my Hungarian neighbour Anna) and *Stories I Want to Tell You in Person* (all completely true stories about my love life and psychics with one made-up element – an Apocalypse Bear). Stuck Pigs Squealing produced *Lally Katz and the Terrible Mysteries of the Volcano*, a play where Canberra was a tropical island and Luke Mullins played the character of Lally Katz, who was sometimes a male detective and sometimes a teenage girl. Brian Lipson played Lion, my childhood stuffed toy.

I'd like to thank the actors who participated in the many developments of this play over the last six years and dramaturgs, Anthea Williams and Louise Gough, and Andrew Eklund from Transgender Victoria for his invaluable consultancy. And my family for not disowning me even though I constantly make them characters and make up stuff about their lives.

A WORD FROM KARATE CONSULTANT, NATSUKO MINEGHISHI

After World War II, Japan was occupied by the US and all martial arts were banned for seven years. With the hope of saving the art, many senseis were sent overseas. The weight of such a mission is unimaginable! It's a credit to these masters that karate is now practiced everywhere, but the tradition is becoming less emphasised. While learning the script, all the performers got into karate immediately. Strange as it may seem, the rigidity of structural training leads to a sense of freedom. Repetitive, often confronting, physical training with the ritual of discipline, respect and honour – this is the world of karate I love to share.

Lally Katz

DIRECTOR'S NOTE

Chris Kohn

Lally first put forward the concept of *Back at the Dojo* in 2010. Finding ourselves with no new project in development, I asked her if there were any stories she was burning to tell. In response, she told me about this idea she had of theatricalising the story of her parents' meeting. She told me about her father Dan's experiences in late 60s and early 70s New Jersey and Kentucky, when he went through a bad time with hallucinogenic drugs, nearly losing his mind, before discovering a new path in life through a chance encounter with a karate dojo, run by a complex and enigmatic sensei. Through this dojo, Dan met Lally's mother Lois. Naturally, I wanted in.

Audiences familiar with Lally's work will know that she frequently draws on elements of her own life in her writing, albeit mostly through an abstracting, "magic realist" lens. Her predilection for personal myth-making is a defining feature of her oeuvre and an important source for her idiosyncratic style and thematic preoccupations. I saw the Dan and Lois Katz narrative as an opportunity to build on Lally's project of mining personal narratives, and to explore some ideas around storytelling and family history, while simultaneously addressing motifs inherent in the narrative – the hedonistic idealism of the post-war West, notions of discipline and intergenerational conflict.

Early iterations of the play included meta-theatrical elements, such as the replaying of recordings of interviews between Lally and her father; at one point Dan Katz himself was going to perform in the play. As is almost always the case with plays developed in a collaborative environment, the force of the narrative asserted itself, demanding its own form. Over six years, it emerged as the play it has become.

One of the aspects that excited me most about the play was the centrality of karate to the storytelling. From the beginning of the process of making the work, this has served as a great foundation, both as a physical discipline and a philosophical approach. We were lucky to find early on Natsuko Mineghishi, who is the Sensei of her own dojo in Melbourne, which shares a lineage with Dan's New Jersey dojo, depicted in the play. Natsuko has provided valuable insight to the play, running the rehearsal room as a working dojo through most stages of its development, providing a highly focused and disciplined creative environment.

As with all my collaborations with Lally over the years, I consider it my job to find a theatrical voice for the story that she brings to the room. Together with our collaborators, we test, prompt, argue and dare each other to push outside of our comfort zones, to eschew easy answers and cliché in pursuit of a greater prize – creating a world on stage as vast, messy, absurd and beautiful as the one that we inhabit.

This collaboration between Stuck Pigs Squealing and Belvoir is the latest iteration of a friendship that began 12 years ago, when we presented *The Black Swan of Trespass* and *The Eisteddfod* as part of the B Sharp independent season. Several Stuck Pigs Squealing creatives involved in *Back at the Dojo* – Lally Katz, Luke Mullins, Jethro Woodward and Richard Vabre – were involved back then. Other regulars, such as Brian Lipson and Mel Page, are also veterans of the Belvoir stage, but this is the first time we have collaborated together here on a main stage production.

We are indebted to the actors who helped to develop this show through several creative processes and whose influence is strongly felt in the final product – Christopher Brown, Jim Daly, Bert La Bonte, Jodie le Vesconte, Zahra Newman, Naomi Rukavina, Luke Ryan, Katherine Tonkin and Mark Leonard Winter. I would like to thank Transgender Victoria, especially Andrew Eklund, for the important role they have played as script consultants, providing invaluable insight into the development of the characters of Patti and Dan.

My contribution to this show is dedicated to Danica, Ariel, Bodhi and Carlo, the loves of my life and my own personal spirit guides. Oss.

Chris Kohn

BIOGRAPHIES

LALLY KATZ Writer

Lally is one of the most-produced playwrights in Australia. Her plays *Stories I Want to Tell You in Person*, starring Lally herself, and *Neighbourhood Watch*, starring Robyn Nevin, were developed and had their world premieres at Belvoir. Belvoir's production of *Neighbourhood Watch* was subsequently presented at Melbourne Theatre Company and the play enjoyed a new production at South Theatre Company of South Australia in 2014 starring Miriam Margolyes. *Stories I Want to Tell You in Person* has been performed in New York, India, Mexico, Brisbane, Adelaide and Albury, and was also adapted for screen by the ABC, with Katz reprising her starring role. Her plays *The Black Swan of Trespass* and *The Eisteddfod* (Stuck Pigs Squealing) were part of Belvoir's B Sharp seasons in 2005 and 2007, and both toured to New York. In 2015, Lally wrote the libretto for the opera adaptation of John Marsden's *The Rabbits*, which was a sell-out hit at the at the Perth International Arts Festival and the Melbourne International Arts Festival. Lally also has a long history of producing work at Malthouse Theatre in Melbourne including *Timeshare, Goodbye Vaudeville Charlie Mudd, A Golem Story* and *Criminology* (co-written with Tom Wright). At Sydney Theatre Company, Lally has written *The Mysteries: Genesis, Frankenstein, Waikiki Palace* and *Hip Hip Hooray*, and for the Melbourne Theatre Company, *Apocalypse Bear Trilogy* and *Return to Earth*. For TV, Lally has written episodes of *Wentworth, The Elephant Princess* and *Spirited*. She has won two Victorian Premier's Literary Awards, a New York International Fringe Festival Award and several Green Room Awards. Lally has been awarded a Churchill Fellowship, a British Council Realise Your Dreams grant and a playwriting grant from The Australian Writers' Foundation.

CHRIS KOHN Director

Chris is making his return to Belvoir after directing *Antigone* in 2008. He served as Artistic Director of La Boite Theatre in 2014 and Arena Theatre Company from 2008 to 2012. For Arena, he commissioned and directed *Mr Freezy, Goodbye Vaudeville Charlie Mudd* and *Moth*, which have enjoyed many seasons around Australia. In 2012, Chris premiered the large scale installation *The House of Dreaming* and developed the new cabaret work *Cautionary Tales for Children* at the Arts Centre Melbourne and Kennedy Centre in Washington D.C. In 2001, Chris co-founded Stuck Pigs Squealing, one of the key forces in the emergence of a new wave of independent theatre in Melbourne. With Stuck Pigs Squealing, he directed shows in Perth, Melbourne, Sydney, Brisbane and New York. His productions of *The Black Swan of Trespass* and *The Eisteddfod* were landmark shows, receiving a host of awards for direction, writing, design and performance. *The Black Swan of Trespass* received awards for Best Direction and Producer's Choice at the 2004 New York International Fringe Festival. Chris directed *Waikiki Hip* for Sydney Theatre Company in 2007 and *The Children's Bach* for Chamber Made Opera in 2008 (nominated for a 2009 Helpmann Award for Best Direction of an Opera). Chris was a Sidney Myer Creative Fellow (2012-13), and has been the recipient of the George Fairfax Memorial Award, an Ian Potter Cultural Trust scholarship and a residency at the Couvent des Recollets in Paris.

FAYSSAL BAZZI Jerry & others

Fayssal's theatre credits include *Ivanov*, *The Government Inspector*, *Food* (Belvoir); *Woyzeck* (B Sharp/Arts Radar); *Timeshare* (Malthouse Theatre); *Look the Other Way*, *The Other Way* (Sydney Theatre Company); *The Motherf**ker With the Hat* (Black Swan State Theatre Company); *I Only Came to Use the Phone* (Darlinghurst Theatre); *The Pigeons*, *Lord of the Flies* (Griffin Theatre Company); *Don Juan in Soho* (New Theatre); *Redemption*, *This Blasted Earth: A Christmas Miracle with Music*, *Poster Girl*, *Sprout* (Old Fitzroy); *All the Blood and All the Water* (Riverside Theatre); *Cross Sections* (Sydney Opera House); *To the Green Fields Beyond*, *Love, Madness and Poetry* (Seymour Centre); and *Empire: Terror on the High Seas* (Bondi Pavilion Theatre). Fayssal's most recent film and TV credits include *Top of the Lake (Season 2)*, *The Elegant Gentleman's Guide to Knife Fighting*, *Tough Nuts*, *Crownies*, *The Strip*, *East West 101*, *Double the Fist*, *Stupid Stupid Man*, *All Saints*, *Emulsion* and *Cedar Boys*. He also features in *Down Under* and *6 Days,* with both films due out in cinemas later this year.

NINA BONACCI Producer – Stuck Pigs Squealing

Nina is an arts producer and manager. In addition to working with Stuck Pigs Squealing, she currently produces Sisters Grimm, one step at a time like this and Melinda Hetzel & Co, among other companies. Nina was Company Manager at Malthouse Theatre for several years, where she enjoyed working with some of Australia's finest artists. Prior to that, she produced and toured contemporary Australian productions nationally and internationally while Associate Producer at Performing Lines, including Back to Back Theatre's *small metal objects* and Stephen Sewell's *Three Furies*. She has worked as Producer at Melbourne International Comedy Festival, Festival Director for Mudfest – Melbourne University's student arts festival; Producer at Keep Breathing, Administration and Development Coordinator at Arena Theatre Company, Marketing Manager at St Martin's Youth Arts Centre, and as Publicist at Miranda Brown Publicity, with clients including Big Day Out and Circus Oz. Nina has participated on the Peer Assessment Panel for Sydney Opera House, on the Next Wave Festival Curatorial Committee, as Chair of visual theatre company Peepshow Inc, and has served on the Platform Youth Theatre Board of Management.

DARA CLEAR Brown belt & others

Dara trained at the Young Gaiety School of Acting in Dublin and at Cygnet Training Theatre in Exeter. He has a B.A. in English and Philosophy from Maynooth University, Ireland. He has been practising Shotokan karate for 24 years and Yang style Tai Chi for 14 years. Dara's theatre credits include *In Real Time* (Brokentalkers); *Don Quixote* (Bred in the Bone); *The Wiremen* (River Productions); *Keep Coming Back* (Stray Dog Productions); *Burning Dreams*, *Good as Gold* (Team Theatre); *The Quest of the Good People* (Pavilion Theatre); *The Suicide of Miss Understood* (Opera Guerillas); *Tomorrow* (Misery Loves Company); and *A Midsummer Night's Dream*, *Romeo and Juliet* (New Theatre). His television and film credits include *Hard Times*, *Fallout* and *Fair City*. Dara's writing includes short fiction and pieces on emotional and psychological wellbeing.

Fayssal Bazzi, Brian Lipson,
Lally Katz & Catherine Davies

Luke Mullins

CATHERINE DAVIES Lois & others

Catherine appeared in Belvoir's Downstairs production of *The Kiss* and will make her Upstairs debut with *Back at the Dojo*. The actress' most recent theatre credits include *Dracula* (co-devised with Little Ones Theatre and Theatre Works); *Dangerous Liaisons* (Little Ones Theatre/MTC Neon/Brisbane Powerhouse/Theatre Works/VCE); *Ground Control* (Next Wave Festival); *Lord of the Flies* (US-A-UM/Malthouse Helium); *sex.violence.blood.gore* (MKA/Tamarama Rock Surfers); and *He Left Quietly* (New York Theatre Workshop). As a key collaborator of Arthur, Catherine co-devised and performed in various projects including *The Myth Project: Twin* (MTC Neon), *Superhero Training Academy*, *Waltzing Wooloomooloo*, and the multi-award winning *Cut Snake*, which toured nationally. She works regularly with Playwriting Australia as an actor and as a facilitator for their Outreach and Lotus (Performance 4A) programs. She has extensive experience developing new Australian work and is an Associate Artist of Milk Crate Theatre. Catherine graduated from QUT with a BFA (Acting) in 2006 and trained at HB Studio, New York in 2010. She's a recipient of the Ashley Wilkie Award for Outstanding Contribution to the Performing Arts.

MEL DYER Stage Manager

For Belvoir, **Mel** has been Stage Manager for *The Great Fire*, *The Dog/ The Cat*, *Is This Thing On?*, *Cain and Abel*, *Angels in America Parts One* and *Two* and *Every Breath*, and Assistant Stage Manager for *Ivanov*, *Peter Pan* (New York tour), *Cat on a Hot Tin Roof*, *Private Lives*, *Death of a Salesman*, *As You Like It*, *Neighbourhood Watch*, *The Seagull*, *The Diary of a Madman*, *Measure for Measure*, *The Promise*, the 2009 Australian tour of *Page 8* and the 2008 tour of *Keating!*. Mel has also appeared on stage for Belvoir in *Ivanov*, *As You Like It*, *Neighbourhood Watch*, *The Seagull* and *Keating!*. Her other credits include Stage Manager for *Lawn*, *Edgar*, *Remember Me*, *Legless* (Splintergroup/ Festspielhaus, Austria); *Roadkill* (Splintergroup/Performing Lines); *Underground* (Dance North/Performing Lines); and *Night Café* (Dance North), and Assistant Stage Manager for *The Golden Age*, *Boys Will Be Boys* (Sydney Theatre Company); *Masquerade* (Griffin/State Theatre Company of South Australia); and *Assembly* (Chunky Move). Mel is a 2007 graduate of NIDA's Production course.

LOUISE GOUGH Dramaturg

Louise is a dramaturg, script editor and development executive. Louise has developed a number of works across narrative, contemporary circus, youth arts, performance and Indigenous theatre, from intimate venues to international festivals. Louise has script or been dramatic advisor on a number of feature films in Australia and throughout Europe. Previous positions Louise has held include Dramaturg in Residence (La Boite Theatre), Literary Manager (Playbox), Editorial Manager (ABC TV Drama and Narrative Comedy), Script Manager (Film Victoria), Literary Fellow (Vineyard Theatre, NYC), Resident Dramaturg (Queensland Theatre Company), Curatorial Advisor (Queensland Performing Arts Centre), and Development (Madman Production Company). Louise works throughout Europe with Sources 2 as an Advisor in their residential feature film development labs and is currently a Development Executive at Screen Australia.

HARRY GREENWOOD Dan (younger)

Harry graduated from the National Institute of Dramatic Art in 2012. For Belvoir, he has performed in *The Glass Menagerie* and *Once in Royal David's City*. Other theatre credits include *Love and Information* (Malthouse Theatre/Sydney Theatre Company) and *Fury* (Sydney Theatre Company). While at NIDA, Harry performed in *Caligula*, *Punk Rock*, *Flutter Kick*, *Rookery Nook*, *Idiot*, *Richard III*, *The American Clock* and *Too Young for Ghosts*. Harry's film credits include Mel Gibson's *Hacksaw Ridge*, *Kokoda* and *8*. His short film credits include *Pacific*, *The Water Diary*, *The Gift*, *The Unlikely Maestro* and *Steve the Chameleon*. For TV, he has appeared in *Old School* and *Gallipoli*.

BRIAN LIPSON Dan (older)

Brian's theatre credits include *The Power of Yes*, *Scorched* (Belvoir); *A Midsummer Night's Dream* (La Boite Theatre); *The Tempest* (Bell Shakespeare); *The Collected Works of Victor Berman* (fortyfivedownstairs); *The Golem Story*, *White Rabbit, Red Rabbit*, *The Goldberg Variations*, *Inside O1* (Malthouse Theatre); *The Crucible*, *Tribes*, *Life Without Me*, *Grace*, *History Boys*, *Dinner*, *Fred*, *Pride and Prejudice*, *Absurd Person Singular*, *The Herbal Bed* (Melbourne Theatre Company); *The Duel* (Sydney Theatre Company/Thin Ice); *Apocalypse Bear Trilogy* (which he co-directed with Luke Mullins for Melbourne Theatre Company); and *Lally Katz and the Terrible Mystery of the Volcano*, *night maybe* (Stuck Pigs Squealing). His solo show *A Large Attendance in the Antechamber* received wide acclaim at festivals in Edinburgh, Sydney and Adelaide, and also toured the USA. His new solo work *Edmund: The Beginning* opened in Melbourne last year and is soon to tour. The opera he directed and wrote with Matthew Hindson, *Love, Death, Music and Plants*, was enthusiastically received in Melbourne in 2003. His play *Berggasse 19 - The Apartments of Sigmund Freud* was a sell-out success when it premiered at the Melbourne International Arts Festival 2005. He has been nominated for eight Green Room Awards and been the recipient of four. Brian's Australian television credits include *Jack Irish*, *The Ex-PM*, *Deadline Gallipoli*, *Miss Fisher's Murder Mysteries*, *Rush*, *Tangle*, *Carla Cametti PD*, *Bastard Boys*, *Nightmares & Dreamscapes*, *Last Man Standing*, *After the Deluge*, *MDA*, *The Secret Life Of Us*, *Thunderstone*, *Blue Heelers* and *Stingers*. His Australian film credits include *Holding the Man*, *Sucker*, *The Book of Revelation*, *The Tragedy of Hamlet Prince of Denmark* and *The Drover's Boy*. He was awarded an Australia Council Fellowship in 2011.

NATSUKO MINEGHISHI Sensei/Karate Consultant

The multi-talented **Natsuko** runs her own karate dojo in Melbourne, teaches singing, and works as a freelance singer and event organiser. She graduated from Melbourne University with a Bachelor of Music (Honours) and a Master of Music Performance. She also received the highest score from Amsterdam Conservatorium for her Graduate Degree in Contemporary Music through Non-Western Technique. Natsuko first studied karate when she was at university. She has been training over 24 years and currently holds her fourth dan black belt degree with Shotokan Karate International Federation (SKIF). In 2012, Natsuko won dual gold medals at the SKIF World Championship. Today, Natsuko is frequently invited to events where she is asked to teach, translate, perform, and coordinate concerts and karate demonstrations. She is also regarded as the first person in the world to have ever been recorded demonstrating a Shotokan Kata while singing a Japanese karate song. Her songs and video recordings are available via iTunes, Spotify and YouTube.

Catherine Davies

Fayssal Bazzi, Luke Mullins,
Harry Greenwood & Dara Clear

Dara Clear, Luke Mullins, Catherine Davies, Harry Greenwood,
Fayssal Bazzi & Brian Lipson

LUKE MULLINS Patti

Luke has previously appeared for Belvoir in *Small and Tired*, *Angels in America Parts One* and *Two*, *The Glass Menagerie*, *Death of a Salesman* and *The Power of Yes*, and in *Thom Pain (based on nothing)* for B Sharp/Arts Radar. His other theatre credits include *Waiting for Godot*, *Little Mercy*, *The War of the Roses*, *Gallipoli*, *The Season at Sarsaparilla*, *The Serpents Teeth*, *Tales from the Vienna Woods* (Sydney Theatre Company); *Long Day's Journey into Night* (Sydney Theatre Company/Artists Repertory, Portland); *The Duel* (Sydney Theatre Company/Thin Ice); *The Eisteddfod*, *4xBeckett*, *Agoraphobe*, *Lally Katz and the Terrible Mysteries of the Volcano*, *Untitled Intentional Exercise*, *Nine Days Falling*, *Apocalypse Bear Trilogy* (Stuck Pigs Squealing); *Cloud Nine*, *The History Boys*, *Oedipus* (Melbourne Theatre Company); *Night on Bald Mountain*, *Autobiography of Red* (Malthouse Theatre); *I Heart John McEnroe*, *The Man with the September Face* (Uninvited Guests); and *Irony is Not Enough: Essay on My Life as Catherine Deneuve* (Fragment 31). Luke has also appeared on TV and in film projects such as the *Holding the Man* (directed by Neil Armfield), and the UK televisions series, *New Blood*, soon to air. In 2013, Luke directed Kit Brookman's *night maybe* for Stuck Pigs Squealing in Melbourne. Luke received a Green Room Award for *The Season at Sarsaparilla* and the George Fairfax Memorial Award for Excellence in Theatre Practice. Luke received a Sydney Theatre Award and the 2014 Helpmann Award for Best Male Actor in a Supporting Role in a Play for *Waiting for Godot*. Most recently, Luke performed the one-person play, *Lake Disappointment* (which he co-wrote with Lachlan Philpott), at Carriageworks. Luke is a graduate of the Victorian College of the Arts.

MEL PAGE Set & Costume Designer

Mel is a costume and set designer for theatre and film, and is a graduate of the Victorian College of the Arts. For Belvoir, Mel has designed costumes for *Jasper Jones*, *Ivanov*, *Seventeen*, *The Dog/The Cat*, *Elektra/Orestes*, *Kill the Messenger*, *A Christmas Carol*, *The Glass Menagerie*, *Nora*, *The Government Inspector*, *Once in Royal David's City*, *Hamlet*, *Angels in America*, *Strange Interlude*, *As You Like It* and *The Promise*, and has designed set and costumes for *Small and Tired*, *Medea* and *Old Man*. Her other costume credits include *Die Tote Stadt*, *Three Sisters*, *Angels in America* (Theater Basel); *The Suicide*, *The Only Child*, *Spring Awakening* (B Sharp/The Hayloft Project); *Les Liaisons Dangereuses*, *Pygmalion* (Sydney Theatre Company); *The Government Inspector*, *Pompeii L.A.* (Malthouse Theatre); *Depth of Field* (Chunky Move); *Complexity of Belonging* (Chunky Move/Melbourne Theatre Company/Melbourne Festival); *Baal* (Malthouse Theatre/Sydney Theatre Company); *Vs. Macbeth* (Sydney Theatre Company/The Border Project); and *The Nest* (The Hayloft Project). She has also designed both set and costumes for *Puncture* (Legs on the Wall); *Venus in Fur* (Darlinghurst Theatre); *night maybe* (Theatre Works); and *Apocalypse Bear Trilogy* (Stuck Pigs Squealing/Melbourne Theatre Company).

OLIVIA SATCHELL Directorial Secondment

Olivia is a writer, director and curator based in Melbourne and Sydney. Her work includes the multi-playwright project *Heart Dot Com* (Tap Gallery) and solo performance work *My Name is Truda Vitz* (Somersault Theatre Company/Tap Gallery). She co-founded the new writing development company Somersault Theatre in 2013 and is the co-curator of the Melbourne monthly performance program Small and Loud. She is studying her Masters of Directing for Performance at the Victorian College of the Arts. In 2016, she assistant-directed *Splendour* (Red Stitch) and *Bright World* (Arthur/Theatreworks). Her play *I sat and waited but you were gone too long* recently received a National Script Workshop with Playwriting Australia.

SHARI SEBBENS Pamela, Connie & others

Shari is a proud Bardi, Jabirr-Jabirr woman, born and raised in Darwin. She is a passionate advocate for Indigenous theatre, especially the development of new and contemporary works. At 19 years of age, Shari was one of ten young artists chosen for SPARK, the Australia Council for the Arts' first theatre mentorship program. In 2006, she was accepted into the Western Australian Academy of Performing Arts (WAAPA) where she completed a Certificate III in Aboriginal Theatre. She then graduated from NIDA's acting program in 2009. She performed in *Radiance* for Belvoir in 2015. Shari's other theatre credits include *The Battle of Waterloo* (Sydney Theatre Company); *The Bleeding Tree*, *Return To Earth* (Griffin Theatre); *Shadow King* (Malthouse Theatre/Darwin Festival); *Lobby Hero* (Tap Gallery); *A Hoax* (La Boite Theatre/Griffin Theatre); *Wulamanayuwi and the Seven Pamanui* (Darwin Festival); and *A Midsummer Night's Dream* (Darwin Theatre Company). Shari was cast in her first film role in *The Sapphires*, which had its world premiere at the 2012 Cannes International Film Festival, and her other film credits include *Teenage Kicks* and *The Darkside*. She has also appeared in the web series *Soul Mates*. Shari is the recipient of the 2012 Graham Kennedy Logie Award for Outstanding New Talent.

KEIREN SMITH Assistant Stage Manager

For Belvoir, **Keiren** has been stage manager on *La Traviata* and assistant stage manager on *Mother Courage and Her Children*, *Radiance*, *Nora*, *Brothers Wreck* and *Once in Royal David's City*. She has an Advanced Diploma in Stage Management from the Western Australian Academy of Performing Arts (WAAPA) and a Bachelor of Arts in Communication and Cultural Studies from Curtin University. Prior to working at Belvoir, Keiren was assistant stage manager with The Australian Ballet for three years, touring domestically and internationally including to Japan and New York, working on many repertoire and new ballets such as *Don Quixote*, *Onegin*, *The Merry Widow*, *Madame Butterfly*, *Coppelia*, *The Nutcracker* and *The Silver Rose*, Alexei Ratmansky's *Cinderella*, Stephen Bayne's *Swan Lake* and Graeme Murphy's *Romeo and Juliet*. Her other credits as assistant stage manager include *Hay Fever* (Sydney Theatre Company); *Solomon and Marion* (Melbourne Theatre Company); Sydney New Year's Eve – Lord Mayor's Party (City of Sydney); and *The Web* and *Much Ado About Nothing* (Black Swan).

RICHARD VABRE Lighting Director

Richard is a freelance lighting designer who has lit productions for Melbourne Theatre Company, Sydney Theatre Company, Malthouse Theatre, Victorian Opera, Windmill Theatre, Arena Theatre Company, National Institute of Circus Arts, the Darwin Festival, Stuck Pigs Squealing, Chamber Made Opera, Rawcus, Red Stitch Actors Theatre, Polyglot, Melbourne Workers Theatre, Aphids, Uninvited Guests, St Martins Youth Arts Centre, and many productions at La Mama. Richard has won four Green Room Awards including the Association's John Truscott Prize for Excellence in Design (2004). He has also been nominated for seven other Green Room Awards.

ANTHEA WILLIAMS Dramaturg

Anthea is Belvoir's Associate Director – New Work. For Belvoir, she has directed *Kill the Messenger*, *Cinderella*, *Forget Me Not* and *Old Man* and has been dramaturg on a number of works including *Mortido*, *Seventeen*, *Samson*, *This Heaven* and *Small and Tired*. Prior to joining Belvoir in 2011, Anthea was Associate Director bushfutures at London's Bush Theatre, where her directing credits include *Two Cigarettes*, *50 Ways to Leave Your Lover*, *50 Ways to Leave Your Lover at Christmas*, *Turf*, *suddenlossofdignity. com*, and the musical *The Great British Country Fete*. Anthea's work toured Britain extensively, including to The Drum Theatre Plymouth, The Ustinov Bath, The Tobacco Factory Bristol, the Norwich Playhouse, North Wall Arts Centre Cambridge and the Latitude Festival. Her other directing credits include *A Question* (nabokov); *The Real You* (SmackBang); and *Quiet* (Fontanel). Prior to working at the Bush Theatre, Anthea was the Co-Artistic Director of SmackBang Theatre Company and the producer of Massive Company, both in Auckland, New Zealand. Anthea trained at the Victorian College of the Arts (Directing) and the University of New South Wales.

JETHRO WOODWARD Composer & Sound Designer

Jethro is a Melbourne-based composer, musician and sound designer recognised for his expansive and highly layered film, theatre and dance scores. A multi-Green Room Award winner and nominee, he has worked with some of Australia's leading major and independent companies including Belvoir, Sydney Theatre Company, Melbourne Theatre Company, Malthouse Theatre, Chunky Move, Arena, Windmill, Melbourne Symphony Orchestra, Rawcus, Stuck Pigs Squealing, Fragment 31, Lucy Guerin, Australian Dance Theatre, KAGE and more. Jethro has won Green Room Awards for *Moth* (Malthouse Theatre/Arena), *Goodbye Vaudeville Charlie Mudd* (Malthouse Theatre/Arena), *Irony Is Not Enough* (Fragment 31), and *The Bloody Chamber* (Malthouse Theatre). He was the Musical Director and Sound Designer for the Helpmann nominated musical *Wizard of Oz* and multi-award winning *Pinocchio* (Windmill). Most recently, he was musical director for *Meow Meow's Little Mermaid* (Sydney Festival 2016).

Natsuko Mineghishi

Fayssal Bazzi & Harry Greenwood

STUCK PIGS SQUEALING

Belvoir is proud to partner with Stuck Pigs Squealing on this co-production of _Back at the Dojo_.

STUCK PIGS
SQUEALING

Stuck Pigs Squealing was established in 2000 as an independent collective of artists dedicated to creating original works of theatre with an emphasis on long-term collaboration, conceptual boldness, formal experimentation and relentless curiosity. The company's repertoire has explored the mythic structures that lie beneath the surface of domestic and suburban reality, receiving critical acclaim and achieving cult status, while immersing audiences into worlds surprising and uncertain.

Productions to date: _tonight I must be brave_ (WA Fringe Festival 2001); _The Architect and the Emperor of Assyria_ (Melbourne Fringe Festival 2001 where it was awarded Best Production of an Existing Text and Festival Director's Choice, B-Sharp in 2002, the International Gay Games Cultural Festival); _4xBeckett_ (Store Room 2002); _The Black Swan of Trespass_ (Melbourne Fringe Festival 2003, New York International Fringe Festival, B-Sharp, Malthouse); _Agoraphobe_ (Next Wave Kickstart 2003); _The Eisteddfod_ (Store Room, New York International Fringe Festival, PS-122 and Ontological, B-Sharp, Malthouse, Brisbane Powerhouse for World Theatre Festival); _Lally Katz and the Terrible Mysteries of the Volcano_ (Theatreworks 2006); _Apocalypse Bear Trilogy_ (Melbourne Theatre Company and Melbourne Festival 2009), _night, maybe_ (Theatreworks 2013). In 2006-7, the company worked with Obie award-winning playwright Mac Wellman and independent company Banana Bag and Bodice in New York and Melbourne, hosted by PS122, Ontological and ArtsHouse. In 2007, they developed _The Poetics of Space_ in Paris. Their work has been the recipient of six Green Room Awards, four Melbourne Fringe Festival Awards and two New York International Fringe Festival Awards.

NOTE FROM TRANSGENDER VICTORIA

TRANS
GENDER
VICTORIA

Congratulations to Stuck Pigs Squealing and Belvoir for their sensitive and co-operative approach regarding trans and gender diverse (TGD) issues. Awareness of TGD people is a part of good human behaviour and treating people with dignity and respect. For TGD people, this includes affirming pronouns (if any) and name the person uses, in service provision having inclusive processes and forms for all genders (such as gender and mailing title), and for doctors and carers being aware of diverse bodies and asking consent to touch body parts. Generally, listen and let TGD people direct our own lives – which is ultimately what we all want. Contact us via www.transgendervictoria.com for more information.

BELVOIR STAFF

18 Belvoir Street, Surry Hills NSW 2010
Email mail@belvoir.com.au Web belvoir.com.au
Administration (02) 9698 3344 Facsimile (02) 9319 3165 Box Office (02) 9699 3444

Artistic Director
Eamon Flack
Executive Director
Brenna Hobson
Deputy Executive Director & Head of Development
Nathan Bennett

ARTISTIC & PROGRAMMING
Associate Producer
Luke Cowling
Associate Director – New Work
Anthea Williams
Artistic Associate
Tom Wright
Associate Artist
Nell Ranney

EDUCATION
Education Manager
Jane May
Acting Education Coordinator
Hannah McBride

ADMINISTRATION
Artistic Administrator
John Woodland
Trainee Administration Coordinator
Anthony Blanch

FINANCE & OPERATIONS
Head of Finance & Operations
Kate Chalker
Company Accountant
Komal Rabadiya
Accounts Administrator
Susan Jack
IT & Operations Manager
Jan S. Goldfeder

BOX OFFICE
Box Office Manager
Tanya Ginori-Cairns
Assistant Box Office Manager
Andrew Dillon
Subscriptions Manager
Jason Lee

FRONT OF HOUSE
Front of House Manager
Ohmeed Ahi
Assistant Front of House Manager
Scott Pirlo

DEVELOPMENT
Acting Philanthropy Manager
Charlotte Bradley
Development Coordinator
Aimee Timmins

MARKETING
Marketing Manager
Amy Goodhew
Marketing Coordinator
Georgia Goode
Communications Coordinator
Cara Nash
Publicity & Public Affairs Manager
Elly Baxter

PRODUCTION
Head of Production
Sally Withnell
Production Coordinator
Eliza Maunsell
Technical Manager
Will Jacobs
Resident Stage Manager
Luke McGettigan
Staging & Construction Manager
Penny Angrick
Staging & Construction Assistant
Brydie Ryan
Costume Coordinator
Judy Tanner
Senior Technician
Caitlin Porter
Commercial Construction Manager
Simon Boyd

SUNDAY FORUM

See the show, and let's talk about it afterwards.

Sometimes the most fascinating part of a theatre-going experience is delving into not just *what* it's about, but *how* it's being done. At Belvoir's Sunday Forums we bring artists and audiences together to peel back the surface and see what's really going on in our plays. We'll chew over the social, the political and the familial. We'll discuss the play, the production – and the glorious space between the two. Serious one month, feisty the next – but always intriguing and you're *always* invited.

We hold a Forum for each of our Upstairs productions. The panellists are made up of both theatre artists and invited guests; you can check our website in advance for a run-down of who will be on and the topic of conversation. You'll have the chance to ask questions, meet your fellow audience members and continue the discussion informally with us in the bar afterwards.

Sunday Forums are **FREE** but we'd like you to book so we can save you a spot. Book online at **belvoir.com.au/sundayforum** or call Box Office. Tweet while you listen using #sundayforum

Back at the Dojo
3pm, 17 July

Twelfth Night
3pm, 4 September

The Drover's Wife
3pm, 16 October

Faith Healer
3pm, 27 November

Girl Asleep
3pm, 18 December

Luke Mullins

BELVOIR
ST THEATRE

Theatricality. Variety of life. Faith in humanity.

Belvoir is a theatre company on a side street in Surry Hills, Sydney. We share our street with a park and a public housing estate, and our theatre is in an old industrial building. It has been, at various times, a garage, a sauce factory, and the Nimrod Theatre. When the theatre was threatened with redevelopment in 1984, more than 600 people formed a syndicate to buy the building and save the theatre. Thirty years later, Belvoir St Theatre continues to be home to one of Australia's most celebrated theatre companies.

In its early years Belvoir was run cooperatively. It later rose to international prominence under first and longest-serving Artistic Director Neil Armfield and continued to be both wildly successful and controversial under Ralph Myers. Belvoir is a traditional home for the great old crafts of acting and story in Australian theatre. It is a platform for voices that won't otherwise be heard. And it is a gathering of outspoken ideals. In short: theatricality, variety of life, and faith in humanity.

At Belvoir we gather the best theatre artists we can find, emerging and established, to realise an annual season of works – new Australian plays, Indigenous works, re-imagined classics and new international writing. Our work travels the country and we regularly take our productions overseas. Audiences remember many landmark productions including *Angels in America, Brothers Wreck, The Glass Menagerie, Neighbourhood Watch, The Wild Duck, Medea, The Diary of a Madman, Death of a Salesman, The Blind Giant is Dancing, Hamlet, Cloudstreet, Aliwa, The Book of Everything, Keating!, The Exile Trilogy, Exit the King, The Sapphires* and *Who's Afraid of Virginia Woolf?*

Belvoir receives government support for its activities from the federal government through the Major Performing Arts Panel of the Australia Council and the state government through Arts NSW. We also welcome and warmly appreciate all philanthropic support.

belvoir.com.au
Artistic Director **Eamon Flack**
Executive Director **Brenna Hobson**

BELVOIR

TWELFTH NIGHT

23 JULY – 4 SEPTEMBER UPSTAIRS

By William Shakespeare
Director Eamon Flack

BOOK NOW
BOOKINGS 02 9699 3444
BELVOIR.COM.AU

NSW | Arts NSW   Australian Government   Australia Council for the Arts

IMAGE: Brett Boardman

BELVOIR DONORS

We give our heartfelt thanks to all our donors for their loyal and generous support.

CREATIVE DEVELOPMENT FUND

$10,000+
Andrew Cameron AM
& Cathy Cameron**
Sherry-Hogan Foundation*
Kim Williams AM & Catherine Dovey

$5,000 - $9,999
Anonymous (1)
Stephen Allen
Anne Britton**
Hartley Cook*
Louise Herron AM & Clark Butler**
Peter & Rosemary Ingle*
Helen Lynch AM & Helen Bauer**
Frank Macindoe *
Doc Ross Family Foundation
Victoria Taylor**

$2,000 - $4,999
Neil Armfield AO**
Jill & Richard Berry
Justin Butterworth & Stephen Asher
John Cary
Janet & Trefor Clayton*
Michael Coleman*
Bob & Chris Ernst
Richard Evans
Lisa Hamilton & Rob White
Michael Hobbs
Victoria Holthouse*
David Marr**
David Robb

$500 - $1,999
Helen Argiris
Richard Banks
Chris Collett
Joanna Collins
Linda English
Phillip English
Timothy Hale
Roey Higgs
Stephanie Hutchinson
Angus Hutchinson
Alec Leopold
Janine Perrett*
Steve Rankine
Penelope Seidler
Alenka Tindale
Sheryl Weil

CO-CONSPIRATORS

$10,000+
Gail Hambly**
Anita Jacoby*
David & Jill Pumphrey
Mark Warburton
Peter Wilson
Cathy Yuncken

THE CHAIR'S GROUP

$3,000+
Judge Joe Harman
Marion Heathcote & Brian Burfitt**

$1,000 - $2,999
Antoinette Albert**
Jill & Richard Berry
Jillian Broadbent AO**
Chris Brown
Jan Chapman AO &
Stephen O'Rourke**
Louise Christie**
Wesley Enoch
Kathleen & Danny Gilbert**
Sophie Guest*
Michael Hobbs*
Hilary Linstead**
Ross McLean & Fiona Beith*
Cajetan Mula (Honorary Member)
Steve Rankine
Alex Oonagh Redmond**
Michael Rose & Jo D'Antonio*
Ann Sherry AO*
Penny Ward*
David & Jennifer Watson**
Kim Williams AM**

B KEEPERS

$5,000+
Robert & Libby Albert**
Ellen Borda*
Constructability Recruitment
Marion Heathcote & Brian Burfitt**
Don & Leslie Parsonage*

$3,000 - $4,999
Anonymous (1)
Bev & Phil Birnbaum**
Anne Britton**
Louise Christie**
Suzanne & Michael Daniel**
Robyn Godlee & Tony Maxwell
Colleen Kane**
S Khouri & D Cross
Chantal & Greg Roger **
Peter & Jan Shuttleworth*
Jann Skinner

$2,000 - $2,999
Claire Armstrong & John Sharpe**
Dr Kimberly Cartwright &
Mr Charles Littrell
Bob & Chris Ernst**
Cary & Rob Gillespie
Peter Graves**
David & Kathryn Groves**
David Haertsch**
John Head**
Jennifer Ledgar & Bob Lim*
Louise Mitchell & Peter Pether
Dr David Nguyen**
Timothy & Eva Pascoe**
Merilyn Sleigh & Raoul de Ferranti
Judy Thomson*
Lynne Watkins & Nicholas Harding*

$1,000 - $1,999
Anonymous (3)
Berg Family Foundation**
Max Bonnell**
Dr Catherine Brown-Watt PSM
Jan Burnswoods
Lloyd & Mary Jo Capps**
Elaine Chia
Jane Christensen*
Jeanne Eve**
Lisa Hamilton & Rob White
Wendy & Andrew Hamlin**
Libby Higgin*
Michael Hobbs**
Avril Jeans**
Kevin & Rosemarie Jeffers-Palmer **
Corinne & Rob Johnston*
Margaret Johnston
A. le Marchant*
Stephanie Lee*
Atul Lele*
Hilary Linstead*
Professor Elizabeth More AM**
K Nomchong SC
Jacqueline & Michael Palmer
Dr Natalie Pelham*
Greeba Pritchard*
David & Jill Pumphrey
Richard & Heather Rasker*
Colleen Roche
Lesley & Andrew Rosenberg*
David Round
Andrew & Louise Sharpe*
Jennifer Smith
Chris & Bea Sochan*
Jeremy Storer & Annabel Crabb
Sue Thomson*
Paul & Jennifer Winch

THE HIVE

$2,500
Anthony & Elly Baxter
Nathan & Yael Bennett
Justin Butterworth & Stephen Asher
Dan & Emma Chesterman
Este Darin-Cooper & Chris Burgess
Joanna Davidson & Julian Leeser
Jeremy Goff & Amelia Morgan-Hunn
Piers Grove
Ruth Higgins & Tamson Pietsch
Emma Hogan & Kim Hogan
Nicola Marcus & Jeremy Goldschmidt
Bruce Meagher & Greg Waters
G W Outram & F E Holyoake
Olivia Pascoe
Andrew & Louise Sharpe*
Michael Sirmai
The Sky Foundation
Peter Wilson & James Emmett

EDUCATION DONORS

$10,000+
Doc Ross Family Foundation
Susie & Nick Kelly
Ian Learmonth & Julia Pincus

$2,000 – $4,999
Anonymous (2)
Ian Barnett*
Andrew Cameron AM & Cathy
Cameron**
Estate of the late Angelo Comino
Ari Droga
Julie Hannaford*
Judge Joe Harman
Olivia Pascoe**

$500 – $1,999
32 Edward St
Anonymous (7)
Len & Nita Armfield
Art House Gallery
Victor Baskir
David Bennett AO & Anne Bennett
AB*
Michael & Colleen Chesterman*
Tracey Clancy
Karen Cooper & Simon Tuxen
Erin Devery
Diane Dunlop*
Veronica Espaliat &
Ross Youngman
John B Fairfax AO & Libby Fairfax
Geoffrey & Patricia Gemmell*
Dorothy Hoddinott AO**
Sue Hyde*
Peter & Rosemary Ingle*
David Jonas & Desmon Du Plessis
Stewart & Jillian Kellie*
Xanthi Kouvatas

Veronica & Matthew Latham
Ruth Layton
Jennifer Ledgar & Bob Lim*
David Marr & Sebastian Tesoriero
Mary Miltenyi
Polese Family
Angela Raymond
Peter & Janet Shuttleworth*
Nawal Silfani
Chris & Bea Sochan*
Kerry Stubbs
Drew Tait
Ingrid Villata
Richard & Sue Walsh
Andrew Watts

GENERAL DONORS

$10,000+
Anonymous (1)
Andrew Cameron AM
& Cathy Cameron**
Ross Littlewood
& Alexandra Curtin*

$5,000 – $9,999
Helen Lynch AM & Helen Bauer**

$2,000 – $4,999
Anonymous (2)
Baiba Berzins*
Brenna Hobson
Anita Jacoby*
Patricia Novikoff*
Lynne Watkins & Nicolas Harding

$500 – $1,999
Anonymous (5)
Victor Baskir
Ian Breden & Josephine Key*
Angela Browne

Dr & Mrs Gil Burton
Trevor Carroll
Tim & Bryony Cox*
Jane Diamond*
Elizabeth Fairfax
Jono Gavin
Peter Gray & Helen Thwaites
Priscilla Guest*
Kim Harding & Irene Miller
Harrison & Kate Higgs*
Dorothy Hoddinott AO**
Iphygenia Kallinikos
Robert Kidd
Daniel Knight
Wolf Krueger & José Gutierrez*
Frans Lauenstein
Dr David and Barbara Millons
Irena Nebenzahl
Anthony Nugent*
Judy & Geoff Patterson*
Dr Natalie Pelham
Kathirasen Ponnusamy*
Leigh Sanderson
Elfriede Sangkuhl
Abhijit & Janice Sengupta
Dr Agnes Sinclair
Eileen Slarke & Family**
Andrew Smyth-Kirk
Dr Titia Sprague
Paul Stein
Mike Thompson
Suzanne & Ross Tzannes AM*
Jane Uebergang
Louise & Steve Verrier
Chris Vik & Chelsea Albert
Sarah Walters*
Louisa Ward & Tim Coen
Elizabeth Webby
Brian & Trish Wright

* 5+ years of giving   ** 10+ years of giving   *** 15+ years of giving

Belvoir is very grateful to accept donations of all sizes. Donations over $2 are tax deductible. If you would like to make a donation or would like further information about any of our donor programs please call our Development Team on 02 9698 3344 or email development@belvoir.com.au

List correct at time of printing.

SPECIAL THANKS

We would like to acknowledge Cajetan Mula, Len Armfield and Geoffrey Scharer. They will always be remembered for their generosity to Belvoir.

These people and foundations supported the redevelopment of Belvoir Street Theatre and purchase of our warehouse.
Andrew & Cathy Cameron (refurbishment of theatre & warehouse)
Russell Crowe (Downstairs theatre & purchase of warehouse)
The Gonski Foundation & The Nelson Meers Foundation (Gonski Meers Foyer)
Andrew & Wendy Hamlin (Brenna's office)
Hal Herron (The Hal Bar)
Geoffrey Rush (redevelopment of theatre)
Fred Street AM (Upstairs dressing room)

BELVOIR SPONSORS

MAJOR SPONSORS

EY
Building a better
working world

WOOLCOTT
RESEARCH

D=N·Y
C I N E M A S

BAKER & McKENZIE

MEDIA PARTNERS

SBS

WORLD
MOVIES

IT PARTNER

NCC

ASSOCIATE SPONSORS

REGENTS
COURT
BOUTIQUE ACCOMMODATION

barton
deakin
Government Relations

*E
P

KEY SUPPORTER

THE
BALNAVES
FOUNDATION

Indigenous theatre
at Belvoir supported
by The Balnaves
Foundation

EVENT SPONSORS

VINI

the devonshire

CELLARMASTERS

Coopers

HUNTER VALLEY
UNIQUE ACCOMMODATION Stays

bourke street bakery

Zahli

PATRICK CATERING

~MOHR~

GOVERNMENT PARTNERS

Australian Government

Australia
Council
for the Arts

NSW
GOVERNMENT

Arts
NSW

YOUTH & EDUCATION
SUPPORTER

AFTT ACADEMY OF FILM
THEATRE & TELEVISION

TRUSTS & FOUNDATIONS

AMP Foundation
Copyright Agency Ltd
Coca-Cola Australia
Foundation
Crown Resorts Foundation

Gandevia Foundation
The Greatorex Foundation
Thyne Reid Foundation
Vincent Fairfax Family
Foundation

SUPPORTERS

Macquarie Group
Thomas Creative
Time Out Australia

**For more information on partnership opportunities please contact our
Development team on 02 9698 3344 or email development@belvoir.com.au**

Correct at time of printing.

ALSO BY LALLY KATZ AND AVAILABLE FROM CURRENCY PRESS

Goodbye Vaudeville Charlie Mudd and Return to Earth

Set in Edwardian Melbourne, *Goodbye Vaudeville Charlie Mudd* is an evocation of a forgotten past—a play about pain and cruel desire; about the need for laughter, the palaces we build for it, and its human cost.

'... a deeply accomplished work: darkly beautiful theatre that resonates in the intimate chambers of the mind.' *The Australian*

Return to Earth edges on the whimsical but is ultimately lyrical and profound. It is a poignant play that tenderly captures the moment, often littered with casualties, when a young person moves from transparency to opacity, from childhood to adulthood—a period of intense loss and confusion.

ISBN: 978-0-86819-938-2

Neighbourhood Watch

And God said: Thou shalt love thy neighbour. He obviously hadn't reckoned on Ana.

Neighbourhood Watch is a glorious comedy about hope, death and pets. It's a classic odd-couple story: opposites attract, and from each other they gain a new understanding. But as the domestic crises accumulate, *Neighbourhood Watch* takes on a sense of enormity in the midst of the ordinary that would make Patrick White proud.

Katz is a true original and in *Neighbourhood Watch* her spirit of curiosity turns optimism into an art form.

Winner of the 2012 Helpmann Award - Best Play

ISBN: 978-1-92500-514-1

ALSO AVAILABLE FROM CURRENCY PRESS

The Great Fire by Kit Brookman

Many years ago, in the 1970s, in pursuit of a good life and a sustainable future, Judith and Patrick built a house in the Adelaide Hills. They raised the kids there. As time wore on, bit by bit, the family drifted both from the house and the dream it was born from. Now it's Christmas, the first grandchild is on the way and all three generations have gathered again. In the tinderbox heat of summer, Judith is at a crossroads: can the life they pursued in the first place come good again?

Warm, funny, deeply felt, *The Great Fire* is the work of a brilliant new writing talent, Kit Brookman. It's a play about family, politics and life, about large hopes, uncertainty and the fading triumph of Australian social democracy. In short, *The Great Fire* is a play about us.

ISBN: 978-1-92500-570-7

Jasper Jones based on the novel by Craig Silvey, adapted by Kate Mulvany

It's summer 1965 in a small, hot town in Western Australia. Overseas, war is raging in Vietnam, Civil Rights marches are on the streets, and women's liberation is stirring – but at home in Corrigan Charlie Bucktin dreams of writing the Great Australian Novel. Charlie's 14 and smart. But when 16-year-old, constantly-in-trouble Jasper Jones appears at his window one night, Charlie's out of his depth. Jasper has stumbled upon a terrible crime in the scrub nearby, and he knows he's the first suspect – that goes with the colour of his skin. He needs every ounce of Charlie's bookish brain to help solve this awful mystery before the town turns on Jasper.

Kate Mulvany's adaptation of Craig Silvey's award-winning novel is wise and beautiful – it features a cast of finely drawn teenagers and grown-ups, all searching for their own kind of truth. A coming-of-age story, *Jasper Jones* interweaves the lives of complex individuals all struggling to find happiness among the buried secrets of a small rural community.

'Whether you know the book or not, this piercing adaptation is very much worth seeing for the way it depicts – and shows ways across – some of the deep and enduring divides in our society.' Jason Blake *Sydney Morning Herald*

ISBN: 978-1-92500-563-9

The Blind Giant is Dancing by Stephen Sewell

Brutality in the workplace, rage in the streets, seething in the home. The vulnerability of political parties when they've forgotten why they're there. The intellectual torpor of modern Australia. How power corrupts.

The Blind Giant is Dancing is an angry and tender depiction of an idealist, Allen Fitzgerald, who becomes so embroiled in a party power struggle that he loses sight of what's at stake.

When it premiered in 1983, *The Blind Giant is Dancing* felt like a sharp slap in the face. Now, in an age of ICAC, Union credit cards, speculative housing bubbles, a pulverised working class and vapid leadership in the 21st century, this Australian classic has lost none of its brute force.

ISBN: 978-1-92500-575-2

www.currency.com.au

Visit Currency Press' website now to:

- Buy your books online
- Browse through our full list of titles, from plays to screenplays, books on theatre, film and music, and more
- Choose a play for your school or amateur performance group by cast size and gender
- Obtain information about performance rights
- Find out about theatre productions and other performing arts news across Australia
- For students, read our study guides
- For teachers, access syllabus and other relevant information
- Sign up for our email newsletter

The performing arts publisher

www.ingramcontent.com/pod-product-compliance
Lightning Source LLC
Chambersburg PA
CBHW050018090426
42734CB00021B/3322